B&G Club pg 52 -
It's a wonderful life

Praise for *Charity Case*

"*Charity Case* is an Apollo program for American philanthropy and the nonprofit sector. Pallotta's understanding of the hamstrung nonprofit sector is poetic and therapeutic. His prescription is sensible and profound. *Charity Case* will inspire its readers with an expansive sense of possibility."
— Robert F. Kennedy Jr.

"*Charity Case* is visionary in its empathy. It sympathizes with the donating public's confusion about how charity really works and with the nonprofit sector's plea to be held to standards that engender trust and grow support. At that intersection lies the promise of a new era of enlightenment about charity and social change."
— Art Taylor, president, Better Business Bureau Wise Giving Alliance

"*Charity Case* takes innovative thinking about the social sector to an entirely new level. Dan Pallotta raises the radical prospect that we can change cultural conventions about charity, making a cause of causes themselves. A powerful call to action."
— Jane Wei-Skillern, adjunct associate professor, Haas School, University of California, Berkeley; lecturer, Stanford Graduate School of Business

"It doesn't occur to Dan Pallotta that standing on the sidelines is an option. And he makes it impossible for the rest of us to stand back. *Charity Case* is a wakeup call for every fundraiser around the world. We are the public champions of philanthropy—it's just that not all of us have been aware of that until now."

— Andrew Watt, president and CEO, Association of Fundraising Professionals

Charity Case

HOW THE NONPROFIT COMMUNITY CAN
STAND UP FOR ITSELF
AND REALLY CHANGE THE WORLD

Dan Pallotta

JOSSEY-BASS
A Wiley Imprint
www.josseybass.com

Published by Jossey-Bass
A Wiley Imprint
One Montgomery Street, Suite 1200, San Francisco, CA 94104-4594—
www.josseybass.com

Author photo by Paiwei Wei

Jossey-Bass books and products are available through most bookstores. To contact Jossey-Bass directly call our Customer Care Department within the U.S. at 800-956-7739, outside the U.S. at 317-572-3986, or fax 317-572-4002.

Wiley publishes in a variety of print and electronic formats and by print-on-demand. Some material included with standard print versions of this book may not be included in e-books or in print-on-demand. If this book refers to media such as a CD or DVD that is not included in the version you purchased, you may download this material at http://booksupport.wiley.com. For more information about Wiley products, visit www.wiley.com.

Library of Congress Cataloging-in-Publication Data

Pallotta, Dan.
Charity case : how the nonprofit community can stand up for itself and really change the world / Dan Pallotta.
p. cm.
Includes bibliographical references and index.
ISBN 978-1-118-11752-1 (cloth); ISBN 978-1-118-22448-9 (ebk);
ISBN 978-1-118-23768-7 (ebk); ISBN 978-1-118-26257-3 (ebk)
1. Charity organization. 2. Nonprofit organizations. I. Title.
HV40.P254 2012
361.7'63–dc23

2012011791

Printed in the United States of America
FIRST EDITION
HB Printing 10 9 8 7 6 5 4 3 2 1

To Annalisa, Sage, and Rider.
May you live in a world that
thinks different about making a difference.

This crime called blasphemy was invented by priests for the purpose of defending doctrines not able to take care of themselves.

—ROBERT GREEN INGERSOLL

Contents

Preface

My previous book, *Uncharitable*, was about how our system of charity undermines the causes we love. This book is about how we can undermine that system. *Uncharitable* was about a problem. This book is about a solution. *Uncharitable* was about our plight. This book is about deliverance. For those of you who haven't read *Uncharitable*, a synopsis is included in Chapter One.

It was right for the problem to occupy center stage in *Uncharitable* so that we could meditate on just how damaging the problem is. I didn't want to propose a bunch of solutions. I'll make an analogy to mourning: when you've lost someone you love, you don't want people trying to cheer you up with platitudes. You just want to grieve and be present to the gravity of what's happened to you. In *Uncharitable*, I wanted to be present to the dysfunction that arises out of our rigid and religious ideas about charity.

In *Uncharitable* I described how the system of values and ethics governing the conduct of charity today is actually a religion that was formalized some four hundred years ago by the early Puritan settlers in New England. I discussed how that system was designed to secure the Puritans' salvation in heaven and avoid eternal damnation in a hell hereafter.

This book is about designing a system that can solve social problems. If we can solve some of the great social problems that have plagued and vexed humankind since the beginning of time, that will be heaven enough. And it will rescue billions of human beings from a hell all too present for them in the here and now.

The Puritans believed that problems like poverty were ordained by God and that they would and should be with us forever. This book is about designing a system of charity that responds to our real capacity to eradicate these problems once and for all—and in our lifetime.

In his 2007 keynote address at the MacWorld Conference, Steve Jobs claimed boldly, "Today, Apple re-invents the phone," and he proceeded to unveil the iPhone. If we can do it with the phone, we can do it with charity.

Let us begin the reinvention of charity. How? By creating a national leadership movement specifically for that purpose.

Unlike many other books written about the sector, this one is not academic. It's not a new theory, and it's not about a new way of thinking about giving. It's an immediately actionable plan to get the public to adopt a new way of thinking about giving. That's a big difference. That Zen monks may have found the key to enlightenment is of no consequence if there's no plan to get everyone enlightened.

Why focus on changing the way the public thinks about charity? Why that lever? Because it's the only lever that really matters. Because the general public donates 75 percent of the

$300 billion given to charity every year. Because elected officials and regulators create public policy and contract guidelines based on what they think the public wants. Because board members are also part of the general public. Because charities base their business strategies on what they think the public wants. And because what the public wants is still based on what the Puritans told them they should want four hundred years ago. The way the public thinks about these things gives rise to the system that obstructs us, so it is appropriate to transform the way the public thinks about these things.

It will not happen by accident. It will happen by the power of our own will and commitment. This book is not about a solution that someone else will put in place. It's not about what I'm going to do. It's not written for "them"—the power brokers, the heads of the gigantic institutional funders, the senators and congressmen and congresswomen, although it is for them too. This book is written for all of us: the executive directors, development directors, executive assistants, program directors, fundraisers, communications staff, medical researchers, clinicians, event coordinators, social workers, finance staff, human resource staff, volunteers, donors—all of us who work, day in and day out, to make this world more human within a system that fundamentally works against us. It's about a solution we will have to put in place and about the things we will need to do to put it in place.

It's a road map for how we will organize the transformation of charity.

"Transformation" is one of those words that has lost all equity and meaning through overuse. It gets conflated and interchanged with the word "change." But change and transformation are not the same. "Transformation" means to transcend form. It requires the surrender of all previous forms and all previous reference points.

Change is a faster caterpillar. Transformation is a butterfly. The purpose of this book is to encourage us to take flight and to show us how.

June 2012

Dan Pallotta
Cambridge, Massachusetts

Special Note

The word profit derives from the Latin *proficere*, which means progress. Thus, the term nonprofit means, literally, nonprogress. Beyond that, it has the distinction of being the only sector whose name begins with a negative.[1] It apologizes for itself before it starts.

The sector could not have a worse name. It sends the public all of the wrong signals, and it is time we changed it. Therefore, with a few exceptions, like in quoted passages or where it serves legal accuracy, I don't use it. (You may ask why it appears on the cover. It's because that's the word in common use today, and my publisher and I wanted to make sure everyone will know what the book is about.)

I instead refer to the sector throughout the book as the humanitarian sector. Others call it the social profit sector, the third sector, the independent sector, or a number of other things. Any one of them is better than nonprofit. Hearing it described repeatedly as something other than "the nonprofit sector" might feel annoying—like it's work just to read it. It feels annoying to me. But that's the way it always feels when you're correcting a bad habit. Next time you think about using the word nonprofit, liken it to a really bad habit like using chewing tobacco. That might help break it.

Charity Case

1

And You Thought Public Perception of Congress Was Bad

Public opinion is a permeating influence, and it exacts obedience to itself; it requires us to drink other men's thoughts, to speak other men's words, to follow other men's habits.

—WALTER BAGEHOT, "THE CHARACTER OF SIR ROBERT PEEL"

The money never gets to the people who need it." That's the familiar refrain we hear whenever the subject of charity comes up in casual conversation.

A Google search for "charities waste money" generates 3.6 million results—about twenty-five times more results than a search for the phrase, "charities use money wisely." It hardly constitutes a scientific inquiry, but it probably means we can conclude that people who don't trust charities outnumber people who do.

Similarly, people's comments in the blogs, articles, and forums picked up on a simple Internet search reveal a pervasive public distrust of how charities conduct their business. One person wrote about not understanding why charities waste money on pens and note pads when they could be using that money to help the cause. Another devised a whole new (and very problematic) approach to giving—circumventing charities entirely—to avoid "charity waste": "I never donate a dime to a huge charity. . . . What I like to do is direct donations into what I call 'micro-causes.' . . . For instance, if the *NY Post* writes about a house burning down in Brooklyn and [about] a now-homeless family —put [the family] up in a hotel. . . . [That way] you know that every dollar is being put to work exactly the way you want it to be."[1]

Other comments, like this one from a watchdog blog, were critical of specific charities: "The American Cancer Society spends 9.6% of its revenue on administrative expenses and another 21.8% on raising more money. Thirty cents out of every dollar you donate won't go towards anything cancer-related."[2] Really? Raising money to make cancer research possible isn't cancer related? Although targeted toward a single charity, the assertion exemplifies the illogical yet widely held view that money not spent directly on what is perceived as "the cause" is money not spent on the cause at all.

Sentiments like these are available prefabricated for anyone in the market for an impassioned opinion on the subject, and they get distributed free of charge by the media and the masses. De Tocqueville said, "In the United States, the majority undertakes to supply a multitude of ready-made opinions for the use of individuals, who are thus relieved from the necessity of forming opinions of their own," or, as a good friend of mine says, people are all too prone to mistake certainty for knowledge.[3] He's right. And because the demand for cheap, prepackaged oversimplifications of complicated subjects is very high and because, in some cases, people are looking for a quick excuse not to give, these off-the-shelf positions proliferate and quickly harden into stereotypes.

As a result, Americans are convinced, in large numbers, that charities waste money—they spend too much on "overhead" (never mind what that word actually means) and too much on executive salaries, offices, hotels, meals, trips, fundraisers, conferences, and staff. In the end, most people believe that the money donated doesn't really go to "the cause." Of course, "the cause" is defined extremely narrowly: if hunger, then soup—but not the spoon, the bowl, the stove, the fundraiser that got the money for the stove, or the postage on the thank-you note sent to the donor who donated the money for the stove. Just the soup molecules themselves.

A History of Suspicion

Studies and history consistently confirm this public sentiment. Documented public distrust of charities dates back to the mid-1800s. People were suspicious then that philanthropy was just a way for the wealthy to "atone" for their success and evade taxes.[4] A few decades later, "charity organization" societies began to develop, not to provide services but to "monitor the aid that was being given and to uncover fraud."[5]

In the 1970s, public concern about fundraising and administrative costs in charities grew.[6] Historian Robert Bremner notes that by the end of the 1970s, "twenty states and numerous county and local governments had adopted laws or ordinances limiting charity solicitations to organizations that could prove a sizable proportion of the collection went for charitable purposes rather than for salaries and administrative costs."[7] (Many of these were subsequently rendered unconstitutional by U.S. Supreme Court rulings.)

Paul C. Light, a professor at New York University's Wagner School of Public Service and an expert on public opinion on the sector, notes that things deteriorated further for charities after the attacks of September 11, 2001, when the media and others jumped all over the Red Cross for the speed and manner with which it disbursed donations to victims.[8] The criticism, predictably, had a huge effect, even though it was unfounded. The *Chronicle of Philanthropy* reported in 2002 that a whopping "forty-two percent of Americans said they had less confidence in charities now than they did before the attacks because of the way charities handled donations."[9]

Six years later, things hadn't improved. In 2008, Ellison Research surveyed 1,007 Americans and found that "sixty-two percent believe the typical non-profit spends more than what is reasonable on overhead expenses such as fundraising and administration."[10] A March 2008 survey by the Organizational Performance Initiative at the Wagner School of Public Service also found that "Americans remain skeptical of charitable performance" and that "estimates of charitable waste remain disturbingly high."[11] Only 17 percent felt charities did a "very good job" running programs and services.[12] The study also showed that an astounding 70 percent of Americans believed that charities waste "a great deal" or "fair amount" of money. Just 10 percent of Americans interviewed thought that charities did a "very good job" spending money wisely.[13] To put that in perspective, even Congress, at its worst, fares better. In November 2011, Gallup reported congressional approval at an all-time historic low of 13 percent.[14]

It's a sad state of affairs when you wish you had the approval ratings of Congress.

A Circular Mess

Despite the abundant evidence that the public believes charities waste a great deal of money, I know of no study—and certainly not one that has ever been distributed to the public—showing that charities actually *do* waste money. I'm not aware of any research showing that charities are ineffective at running programs or that they spend more than is reasonable on fundraising and administration, systemically or otherwise. Indeed no logical standard exists for what is reasonable.

I come from this sector. I have worked very closely with many dozens of humanitarian organizations for over three decades. I have worked with hundreds of leaders and professionals inside the sector. And I can tell you that there is no legitimate reason for so many people to have such a low opinion of charities. Robert Kennedy once said, "One fifth of the people are against everything all of the time."[15] If one-fifth of the people said they thought charities waste a lot of money, I wouldn't be concerned. But 70 percent?

At the heart of this low public opinion is the power of suggestion. The word we hear most often when it comes to assessing charities is "overhead": low overhead, high overhead, "ask about overhead," overhead ratings, and everything-else-overhead. Now, if I tell you not to think of an elephant in a cocktail dress, you won't be able to get the image out of your head. Similarly, if the first word that comes to mind when you think about charity is "overhead," and if you are programmed to associate overhead with waste, it follows that waste and charity will become synonymous to you and the rest of the culture.

How do we change this?

Actually it's not clear that public opinion is what we should be trying to change. Low public opinion is a reflection of deeper problems: the sector's apparent inability to move the needle on huge social problems. So asking how we change public opinion is a little like looking at an X-ray that shows you have a tumor and asking how you fix the X-ray. But that's not a perfect analogy because in the case of charity, low public opinion means lower contribution levels, which further inhibits our ability to address huge social problems. To continue the analogy, in the case of charity, the X-ray actually has the ability to make the tumor worse.

When we peel back the layers to examine how public opinion influences charities' behavior, we see that it's a circular mess:

- Charities' fear of public disapproval pressures them to cater to public prejudices—mainly lowering overhead, that is, administrative salaries, fundraising investment, marketing expenditures, and so on.
- The more charities give the public what it wants—low "overhead"—the less those charities can spend educating the public about what they actually do. And the public considers any effort by charities to educate them about what the charities actually do to be wasteful overhead to begin with.
- The less the sector educates the public, the lower the public's opinion of the sector remains.
- The more that charities give the public what it wants—again, low overhead—the less they can grow and therefore the less significant their long-term achievements. Long-term achievements require short-term spending, which yields zero short-term results but increases short-term overhead—which the public abhors.

- The less dramatic the sector's long-term results are, the lower the public's opinion of it.

These conditions are not new. For hundreds of years, charities have been forced to follow a rule book that doesn't allow them to spend money on the things they need to achieve real change. Both despite this frugality and because of it, they are then accused of being wasteful. The humanitarian sector is not innocent in this. It has allowed itself to be victimized. In fact, it can be relied on to allow itself to be victimized.

The sector must reject the role of victim. We must work to improve the sector's public image while simultaneously having the courage to spend money on the things we need to create real change. This will, ironically, have the effect of improving public opinion. Positive public opinion and effecting real change are inexorably linked—and they are at the heart of our dreams for humanity.

This book is about finding the way forward to make our dreams for humanity a reality. It's about confronting the four-hundred-year-old rule book by which all organizations fighting for worthy causes—from disease to poverty to injustice—are forced to play. It's about retiring it—putting it in a museum alongside fossils of the earliest known vertebrates and diagrams of the sun revolving around the earth.

We need a civil rights movement for charity—and this book is about how we start one.

How I Got Here

Forensic investigation of structural dysfunction in social change wasn't what I originally intended to do with my life. I wanted to be a goalie in the National Hockey League. Then I wanted to be the next Bruce Springsteen. But I had neither the reflexes for the former nor the melodic prowess for the latter. And in any event, I got distracted from both pursuits during my first year in college, when I began to learn for the first time about the numbers of people dying of hunger. I can still remember the 1980 statistics: 15 million human beings dying every year of hunger and hunger-related disease, two-thirds of them children. Millions of kids dying every year of diarrhea? For a kid used to contemplating hockey pucks, it was a staggering figure. A staggering thought.

This was around the time the Hunger Project was launched by Werner Erhard, the creator of the est Training. The project's goal was audacious: to end hunger by the year 2000. Now, I was eight years old when Neil Armstrong walked on the moon. The idea that we could get to the moon by saying we were going to do it—the sheer power of declaration—was and remains the most exciting thing in the world to me. So when Erhard said we could end world hunger by saying that we were going to do it, I was hooked.

The Hunger Project did not meet its goal of ending hunger and starvation within twenty years. But it started the conversation that no one else was having: the conversation that will eventually end hunger in our lifetime. It said, "We can do this—we can end this." The conversation until then had been limited to, "Eat your food because there are people starving in the world," or, "We have to help people in whatever little way we can." It was a timeless conversation resigned to the persistence of the problem, summarized four hundred years ago by Puritan leader John Winthrop in his famous sermon, "A Model of Christian Charity": "God Almightie in his most holy and wise providence hath soe disposed of the Condicion of mankinde, as in all times some must be rich some poore, some highe and eminent in power and dignitie; others meane and in [submission]."[16] The Hunger Project said, *Screw that. Hunger is unacceptable. It's time to talk about eradication.*

Today, as a result of changing that conversation, we see initiatives like the United Nations' Millennium Development Goals, which call for achieving a series of benchmarks for tackling extreme poverty by 2015. We see Share Our Strength, calling for the end of child hunger in five years; Bono's ONE Campaign calling on us to save 4 million children's lives within five years;[17] and many other similar examples.

Ralph Waldo Emerson once wrote that "our age is retrospective. . . . It writes biographies, histories and criticism. The foregoing generations beheld God and nature face to face; we, through their eyes. Why should not we also enjoy an original relation to the universe?"[18] The Hunger Project transformed our thinking about hunger from being retrospective to being original. It could be our own.

This was a bigger idea to me than being a goalie in the NHL.

In 1980 I became the chair of the undergraduate Harvard Hunger Action Committee. The committee organized two campuswide fasts each year. That meant we'd ask every kid at school to give up dinner on a specific night, and for every kid who said yes, the University Food Services would give about two dollars to Oxfam America. Each fast raised about two thousand dollars.

We weren't going to end hunger in twenty years that way. I wanted to do something bigger. Two years later, a big idea came to me: get a large group of students to bicycle across the entire continental United States to raise money and awareness for the end of hunger. That was big. It was terrifying. Terrifying was what I was looking for.

By the summer of 1983, my co-chair, Mark Takano, and I had recruited thirty-eight people for our Ride for Life journey across America. Thirty-nine of us took a six-hour flight from Boston to Seattle and spent the next sixty-nine days bicycling 4,256 miles from Seattle to Boston. We met amazing people and experienced the true generosity of Americans. We raised about eighty thousand dollars for Oxfam America, appeared on TV and radio stations all over the country, and arrived home physically, spiritually, and emotionally spent. We had given the most we could for a cause that we cared about deeply.

I remember thinking, *Wow! Would I love to do this kind of thing for a living.* But then that familiar little voice of cynicism that haunts us all from time to time immediately chimed in to tell me that that was a stupid idea. I listened to it, went to work in the Massachusetts State Senate, and hated it. It seemed to me to be an institution committed to doing nothing.

This was also a time of personal turmoil for me. I was coming to terms with the fact that I am gay. I had been interested in a career in politics but figured then, that because I am gay, that was never going to happen.

So I headed to Los Angeles, in part to escape myself, in part to see if songwriting and music could be an outlet for my desire to make a difference. But then the AIDS epidemic hit with full force. Back then it was like a smart bomb aimed at two generations of gay men. And if I'd been born a year earlier, I probably wouldn't be alive today. I had the advantage of learning about AIDS from the media, which was beginning to report on it right before I became sexually active. People born a year earlier weren't so lucky. I can count on one hand the number of gay friends I have in their sixties and seventies. Those two decades of men were wiped out.

Tragedy without modern precedent was all around us, and yet it felt as if there was nothing big anyone could do about it except wear a red ribbon or go to an AIDS gala dinner. I didn't feel like sitting in a hotel banquet room or dabbling in symbolism. I found myself feeling that same helplessness I'd felt in college in the face of hunger. For a while, I thought about organizing another journey—a seven-day pilgrimage on bicycles from San Francisco to Los Angeles. But I just sat on it. I was too depressed and demoralized to do anything about it.

Then I saw the movie *Alive* about the Uruguayan rugby team whose plane went down in the Andes and who, after ninety days, with the world having given them up for dead, breached those terrifying mountains and got themselves rescued. Something in me was awakened. I left the movie theater and a voice not my own said to my friend, Ritch, "That's it. We're going to do the AIDS Ride."

The rest, as they say, is history.

A New Industry

The first event we organized, California AIDS Ride, was a seven-day, six-hundred-mile ride from San Francisco to Los Angeles. Four hundred seventy-eight people rode, and we netted $1,013,000—much more than we'd anticipated—for AIDS services at the Los Angeles Gay & Lesbian Community Services Center.[19] We began organizing AIDS Rides all over the nation. Soon after, we created a three-day pilgrimage for breast cancer: sixty miles from Santa Barbara to Malibu. This time participants walked. That first breast cancer event was four times as successful as the first AIDS Ride, netting over $4 million.[20] We began organizing those all over the country. Then we created journeys for AIDS vaccine research, called the AIDS Vaccine Rides, and then for suicide prevention, called the Out of the Darkness walk. We started doing events in more distant locations—Alaska, Canada, Europe, and Africa. In the process, I founded a company called Pallotta TeamWorks, and we created a whole new category of civic engagement—the long-distance fundraiser and the long-distance life changer—which to date has raised in excess of $1.1 billion for important causes and given new meaning to the hundreds of thousands of people who have participated in them.

In the first eight years, 182,000 people walked or rode in one of our events, over 3 million people donated, and $581 million was raised—more money raised more quickly for these causes than any other events in history.[21] In 2002 we netted $81 million after all expenses—an amount equal to half of the annual giving of the Rockefeller Foundation at the time.

So, it turned out, you *could* make a living taking people on the journey of their lives.

Our company grew to about 350 full-time people in sixteen U.S. offices. Harvard Business School conducted a case study on us. We developed unique capacities for organizing large-scale, multi-day civic events:

- A sixty-person logistics touring team made up of riggers and carpenters and other professionals who would build the mobile cities—which consisted of thousands of tents, multiple command centers, giant dining tents, and other capital equipment to stage the events and care for the walkers and riders for days on end
- Our own in-house fifteen-person ad agency and environmental graphics department with media buyers, designers, traffic

managers, a published poet, world-class photographer, composer, and state-of-the-art recording studio
- A sixty-station in-house call center for customer relationship management, staffed largely by former participants and equipped with state-of-the-art predictive auto dialers and integrated customer relationship management software
- A sophisticated donation tracking system monitoring some $170 million a year in contributions
- The most dedicated and inspiring staff ever assembled for anything
- A multimillion-dollar line of credit that allowed us to launch new events without charities having to risk any of their capital

We did this all for a fixed fee that averaged just 4.01 percent of donations—about the same amount banks and credit card companies charge just to process the donations. One hundred percent of every donation went directly to charities, which then reimbursed us for expenses.

We challenged convention on many levels—not for the sake of being unconventional but because convention, to us, clearly didn't work. In fact, it screwed things up. It minimized potential at every turn. We did what we believed would work: we advertised our events the way Apple advertises iPads. We hired great executives and paid them well—not millions, but $300,000 or $400,000 annually. We provided an exceptionally high level of customer service both before the events and during them. Our literature and materials were gorgeous. We did things about which someone could say, "Well, you could have saved more money for the cause by not doing that" but that we felt contributed to greater participation and more contributions in the long run.

And we integrated all of this into one public-facing brand that challenged the notion that you should not be able to do good and do well at the same time. But there was no vernacular for that back then. Phrases like *social innovation*, *social entrepreneurship*, and *social enterprise* either hadn't been coined or were not yet widely used. There was no *Stanford Social Innovation Review*, no Social Enterprise Program at Harvard Business School.

When you're very successful and you're challenging convention, you attract critics. A few people with loud voices can be counted on by the media to hurl insults and accusations at you with tremendous consistency and conviction. Despite the fact that fifty thousand participants think you're doing everything right, one person who has no direct experience of the events but writes for a big newspaper calls you "controversial," and it becomes a self-fulfilling prophecy. Our experience followed the pattern, and we became "controversial."

The ultimate result was that in 2002, our largest partner, the Avon Products Foundation, appropriated our Breast Cancer 3-Day idea and model and set out to produce long breast cancer walks on its own.[22] Avon's intention to compete with the 3-Days head-on spooked the new charitable partner we had lined up to be the beneficiary of the events for 2003. That new partner backed out at the last minute, after four months of preparations, and we went out of business overnight. We subsequently sued Avon for breach of contract and won—but the arbitration took three years, and our victory came far too late to put the company back together again. Avon's 2003 experiment was tragic in terms of its ability to make breast cancer research grants. Its net revenues available for making grants plummeted from $70.9 million with us in 2002 to $11.1 million when it tried the events on its own in 2003—a $59.8 million negative variance in one year.[23] In an apples-to-apples comparison, costs actually rose as a percentage of revenues.[24]

Over the years of producing these events and successes and then enduring all of the criticism and watching our dedicated staff endure it, I began realizing that there was something fundamentally wrong about the context in which people were trying to create social change. Critics were attacking this charitable endeavor for doing things that businesses are encouraged to do every second of the day and for "causes" that are far less urgent. It struck me not only as illogical but as unjust and, ultimately, destructive. I began cataloguing everything I was observing—storing it away in my head. Over time I began to see a holistic web of illogic that was fundamentally undermining society's ability to achieve social change. And I could see that people were literally religious about it. I decided to write a book about it.

The result was *Uncharitable.* In it I codified everything I had been observing over the previous decade. I described the two rule books that exist, one for charity and one for the rest of the economic world.

At first it was a hard sell. After probably forty rejections from various publishers, Tufts University Press agreed to publish it in 2008.

A Discriminatory Rule Book

This separate rule book by which the humanitarian sector must abide discriminates against the sector—and all those it seeks to help—in five big areas:

1. *Compensation.* We let the for-profit sector pay people a competitive wage based on the value they produce without limit.

But we don't want people making money in charity. Want to make $50 million selling violent video games to kids? Go for it. But if you want to pay the right leader half a million dollars to cure kids of malaria, you and the leader are parasites yourselves.

2. *Advertising and marketing.* We let business advertise until the last dollar no longer produces a penny of value, but we don't like to see charitable donations spent on advertising. So charities can't build retail demand for donations to their causes. Budweiser is all over the Superbowl. AIDS and Darfur are always absent.
3. *Risk taking in pursuit of new donors.* It's okay if a $100 million Disney movie made in pursuit of new moviegoers flops, but if a $5 million charity walk doesn't show a 75 percent profit in year 1, it's considered suspect. As a result, charities shy away from unproven, large-scale community fundraising ideas. This means they can't develop the powerful learning curves the for-profit sector can.
4. *Time horizon.* Amazon.com could go for six years without returning any money to investors in the interest of a long-term goal of building market dominance. But if a charity has a long-term goal that doesn't yield short-term direct services, it's scandalous.
5. *Profit.* Business can offer profits to attract investment capital. But there's no such vehicle for charity. So the "nonprofit" sector is starved for growth capital.

If you put these five things together—you can't use money to attract talent, you can't advertise, you can't take risks, you can't invest in long-term results, and you don't have a stock market—then we have just put the humanitarian sector at the most extreme disadvantage to the for-profit sector on every level, and then we call the whole system charity, as if there is something incredibly sweet about it. Charity could not be undermined with more reverence paid to the notion of something noble.

The catastrophic effects of this separate rule book are sobering. Since 1970, the number of nonprofit organizations that have crossed the $50 million annual revenue barrier is 144. The number of for-profits that have crossed it is 46,136.[25] Eighty-eight percent of the nonprofit organizations in the United States have budgets under $500,000,[26] and only 1 percent have budgets greater than $1 million.[27] This is the crux of the matter. These organizations are dealing with problems of massive proportions, and our rule book prevents them from achieving anywhere near commensurate scale. All the scale goes to Coca-Cola and Burger King.

This discriminatory rule book comes from old Puritan ideas. The Puritans came to the New World for religious reasons, but they also came because they wanted to make a lot of money. They were aggressive capitalists. They formed the Massachusetts Bay Colony as a corporation and were accused of extreme profit-making tendencies by the other colonists. But at the same time, they were Calvinists, so they were taught, literally, to hate themselves. They were taught that self-interest was a raging sea that was a sure path to eternal damnation.

This created a real problem for these people. Here, they had come across the sea to the New World to make a lot of money, but making money would get them sent directly, immediately, and permanently to hell. They reconciled these conflicting values through their system of charity. Charity became an economic sanctuary where they could do penance for their profit-making tendencies. So how could they make money in charity if charity for making money? The Puritans created two where there was only ever one. The merchants, rpenters of the world got free market practice, and nd all who served them) got this religion we call ereby pretty much everything that worked in the marke as banished. We are still stuck with this system today. Self-deprivation is still the prescribed path to social change.

The Question We Have to Stop Asking

These Puritan ideas are held in place today by this one simplistic question: "What percentage of my donation goes to the cause versus overhead?" where we want the amount going to "the cause" to be very high and the amount going to "overhead" to be very low. It makes sense if you don't think about it too much, but with a little reflection, you begin to understand that this method is deeply flawed in at least three critical ways.

First, it makes us think that overhead is not part of the cause. But it absolutely is. Unless there's fraud going on (and if there's fraud going on, no one is going to report it in line item detail on their Form 990), then every dollar that a charity spends in good faith is directed toward advancing the cause in whatever way it believes the cause can best be advanced. Overhead is a phantom. Then what about waste? Doesn't this question uncover waste? No, it doesn't even do that. Money can be wasted in any part of the service delivery chain. Waste is not the exclusive domain of overhead. What good is it to know that 95 percent of your donation goes to the cause if you don't know that all of the money going to the cause is being wasted?

Second, the notion that overhead steals from the cause forces charities to obsess over keeping short-term overhead low at the expense of actually solving problems. If our message to charities is, "My donation to you depends on your keeping overhead low," then what we will get is low overhead, or the appearance of it. Solving social problems becomes a secondary matter because no one's livelihood depends on it.

Third, ironically, the question of overhead gives donors really bad information:

- It tells nothing about the quality of the charity's work. A soup kitchen can tell you 95 percent of your donation goes to soup, but you will never know if the soup is rancid because the overhead ratio contains no information about the soup.
- It doesn't tell how the charity defines the cause. The more broadly the charity defines it, the higher the percentage it can report. Let's say that you donate to a breast cancer charity that tells you 90 percent of your donation goes to the cause. You think the cause is breast cancer research. But the charity defines the cause as fundraising for breast cancer, education about breast cancer, *and* breast cancer research. In reality, only 50 percent of your donation goes to breast cancer research. The practice of stretching the definition of the cause is rampant in our sector because charities know we want low overhead.
- It leads donors to discriminate unknowingly against less popular causes, because these causes have to put more money into fundraising and promotion. They need to be known before anyone will give them money. And getting known costs money. A cause like breast cancer, where one out of every two people in the world is at risk, doesn't have to do that kind of spending.
- It gives the wrong overhead figure because it measures overhead against the wrong result. For example, let's say Jonas Salk

t $10 million to raise $20 million to find a cure for polio. ... divide the $10 million he spent into the $20 million he raised and say he had 50 percent overhead. But raising $20 million was not his result. His result was a cure for polio. If you divide $10 million into the value of a cure for polio—tens, maybe hundreds of billions of dollars—his overhead was a statistical zero.

If It's Such a Bad Question, Why Do We Keep Asking It?

We ask the question because we are trained to ask it. We have been trained by watchdog agencies, state attorneys general, and the media, all of which reinforce each other.

Worse, we are trained to ask this question by the charities themselves, which place the watchdog seals of approval on their Web sites. To get one of these seals, they have to have low overhead. And in some cases, they have to pay for the seal—an expense they have to book as overhead!

When the charities place these seals in prominent places on their Web sites, they are signaling to the general public that overhead is the smart thing to ask about. And since many of them focus on keeping overhead low above all else, or accounting for it in a way that allows them to report it as low, the overhead measure is in their best interest. But it may not be in the best interest of their community or donors. What good is low overhead and organizational stability if we're not solving the problems for which we were chartered?

People in the Humanitarian Sector Crave a New Direction

Since *Uncharitable* was released in 2008, I have given over a hundred and twenty presentations on it to about fifty thousand people in twenty-nine states and seven countries. I've flown nearly a quarter of a million miles doing it. I have spoken to small classes in nonprofit management at Harvard, Stanford, Tufts, Wharton, Brown, and many other universities and to large audiences gathered at annual meetings for the Council on Foundations; the Philanthropy Roundtable; the Southeastern Council on Foundations; Washington, D.C., Grantmakers; Inside NGO; and many others. I have spoken at institutional funders' offices like the Gates Foundation and the Hewlett Foundation, and at leadership meetings for the Boys and Girls Clubs, YMCAs, associations of children's hospitals, and many others. I also write a weekly blog on these issues for *Harvard Business Review* online.

I didn't anticipate the magnitude of the response—the extent to which people would ask me, "What do we do about this? How do I get involved? Where do I sign up?" After every talk I gave, there was a line of people waiting to vent their frustrations with the constraints under which they work and tell me how for years they had been thinking some of these same things but had never heard them articulated as one codified whole.

I didn't expect to discover that the cause of causes themselves is an idea whose time has come. The millions of hard-working people who have dedicated their lives to alleviating suffering and injustice are fed up with suffering injustice themselves. They are tired of being misunderstood, tired of working for artificially suppressed wages, tired of defensively responding to questions about their salaries and about overhead from people who haven't the slightest idea of the realities under which they work. They are tired of being second-guessed by board members driving from the back seat, tired of being asked to solve the most vexing social problems with inadequate resources to make even a scratch on them.

And they are tired of being told to "act more like a business" by businesspeople who refuse to allow them to use any of the real tools of business—adequate resources, to begin with.

Here's a representative sample of some of the hundreds of e-mails and comments I've received from individuals on the front lines:

"I'm signing on as a soldier for sector-wide change. As an industry, we need to retrain the American public on how to evaluate who they're giving to and why."[28]

"I can't remember being as excited about the non-profit world since I began working in this sector."[29]

"I feel at once enraged and empowered."[30]

"I couldn't be more excited that someone is not just advocating, but shouting about the things you've been writing concerning non-profits and the erroneous ways in which people view them."[31]

"You articulated many of the things I find so frustrating about the non-profit world."[32]

"You articulated thoughts that have been bubbling below the surface for this fundraiser for some time. I work at an organization that spends so much time telling our donors about our overhead ratio, as if that were the best reason to give, thereby negating our core mission—making a real change in the community."[33]

"Count me in, Dan! . . . I'm fired up!!"[34]

This recognition that things need to change and the yearning for that change to occur came not only from frontline practitioners but from sector leaders, institutional funders, and leaders of organizations. In a presentation I did at the Bill and Melinda Gates Foundation, one program officer thanked me for raising these issues. She was frustrated about a 15 percent limit on overhead on her grants and the fact that she has to get grantees to recategorize expenses to fit the rule.

Another executive at the Gates Foundation at the time wrote to me:

> I want to say how much I appreciate your blog on giving donors what you think they want. . . . Charities constantly sell themselves short by conforming to donor fads and framing of issues or adapting themselves to the latest government or foundation reformulation of strategy. The symbiotic relationship of donor and recipient has proved to be sustainable and perpetuating—to the detriment of vital social issues.[35]

Paulette Maehara, then president of the Association of Fundraising Professionals, which represents thirty thousand members in 222 chapters throughout the world, wrote to me after a speech in Canada:

> The sector has fallen into a trap we created. By focusing on what we DON'T spend, and not on what has been accomplished, we have completely missed the mark in our messaging. We are part of this problem and it's up to us to educate our way out of it.[36]

Undergraduates, graduate students, and recent graduates were similarly frustrated by the existing state of affairs and pumped by the message. A colleague wrote to tell me about a friend:

> She's in the midst of an MBA program at Berkeley/Columbia . . . and decided to go back to school because she can't stand the poverty culture of the nonprofit sector and says that the [sector] . . . doesn't know how to capitalize its own projects.

> She started out in the for-profit world and has really had a hard time acclimating to the nonprofit worldview.[37]

The overwhelming response to *Uncharitable* made me realize we've reached a tipping point. John Kennedy famously said, "Ask not what your country can do for you. Ask what you can do for your country." Clearly there has never been a lack of people asking what they could do—for their country or their sector. But there's been no effective response.

My best advice in *Uncharitable* was that people in our sector need to have courage. They have to speak out. But that is easier said than done. The stakes are high for an individual. People feel isolated at every level. Everyone worries about job security. Grantees are afraid to talk to institutional funders for fear that it will put their grants at risk. Program officers at foundations have presidents to respond to. Staff members have executive directors to answer to. Presidents at foundations and humanitarian organizations have boards to answer to, and while they may realize that much higher investment in leadership, fundraising, staff training, and retention will enlarge the organization, it is of no moment if putting it into practice gets them fired. Boards feel they have the public, the media, and regulatory authorities to respond to. No board member wants to be the lone champion of a countercultural assault on overhead ratios or low executive compensation. They don't want their organization losing Charity Navigator stars on their watch. They don't want a sensational media investigation because they hired a well-paid executive director.

Courage is still the answer. But courage is easier to muster in numbers. We need to band together. In each other we will find courage.

We Need a National Leadership Movement

It's time to develop a unifying strategy and path forward. For this, we need a leadership movement. Its charter must be to

- *Speak.* It must take the question to the public: How serious are we about solving entrenched social problems? And then it must aggressively educate people about the realities of what it will take to solve them. It must teach the public to think differently about value: the value of investment in leadership, in marketing, fundraising, and expansion. It must teach new ways of thinking about risk—specifically, about the risks of never risking anything. It must teach the public why our theories of transparency and efficiency are broken and undermine the very values they purport to uphold.
- *Train.* It must methodically train the media and regulatory authorities about these issues. And it must provide tools for the training of board members and major and retail donors.
- *Respond.* It must aggressively respond to sensational and inaccurate media stories whenever and wherever they arise.
- *Aggregate.* It must aggregate opinion and ideas and communicate these en masse to foundations. It must start telling foundations together, and regularly, the truth that we have been too afraid to speak on our own. It must pull heads out of the sand.
- *Make legislative history.* It must gather all of the fragmented ideas for structural change, statutory change, and changes in the tax code into one sweeping and proactive piece of legislation.
- *Build.* As part of a legislative act, it must build a mechanism that will give the public—on a complete, objective, and

regularly updated basis—the rich information on the nation's charities that the public needs but has never had. It must build an agency for the distribution of accurate information because without it, no market can function properly.

- *Litigate.* It must challenge federal, state, and local statutes that violate the First Amendment and other rights of the humanitarian sector when they force the sector to speak in the language of administration-to-program ratios.
- *Measure.* It must measure its own impact at every conceivable opportunity. How many media outlets did we train this week? What impact did we have on them? How many board trainings did we do this month? What are the attitudes of the trainees a month later? How are we tracking along a critical path to construct legislation? How are our ads moving our public opinion polls?
- *Bind.* It must organize all of the people who are excited by these ideas in their own communities. By *organize*, I mean bring together, excite, inspire, and engage—give people meaningful things to do that make a clear impact. I mean introduce people to one another. Create new bonds.

No such movement currently exists. There are movements afoot, but they focus on other things. The venture philanthropy movement is searching for innovative charitable programs. The social entrepreneurship movement is training those interested in new ways of combining doing well with doing good. The social capital movement is trying to fund new ventures and has all but written off philanthropy and the humanitarian sector. The impact assessment movement is aimed at the very specific goal of measurement, without an eye on distribution or the larger context in which the measurement will occur. None of these are aimed at correcting structural dysfunction, cultural prejudice, or public illiteracy.

In addition, the social change community and its leadership are fragmented. Our discussions are siloed. We are a motley assortment of institutional funders, charity executives, academics, medical researchers, major donors, professional fundraisers, the family foundation community, institutional investors, social investors, celebrity do-gooders, and the government—the list goes on—and each group has its own segregated annual conference—TED, ARNOVA, Social Enterprise World Forum, Council on Foundations Annual Meeting. There are dozens, if not hundreds, of separate large conferences on social change.

Given the challenges of coordinating activity within the existing dysfunctional framework, it is inconceivable that the current structures could reinvent the framework itself.

Announcing the Charity Defense Council

In *Uncharitable*, I tried to state the problem. Now it's time to get to work solving it. Enough talking about what we need. I want to tell you about what we have. We have an entity. It has a mission. It has a purpose. It has plans. It's called the Charity Defense Council. And it needs you.

The Charity Defense Council was incorporated in Massachusetts in March 2011 and has received its tax-exempt status from the U.S. Internal Revenue Service. As an initial charter, this is what we will do:

- Act as an anti-defamation league for the sector.
- Enlighten the public through paid advertising and media with a whole new conception of charity.

- Gather the best thinkers in the country to design a national civil rights act for charity and social enterprise that would support all of our best new ideas and wipe the slate clean of the old, fragmented, reactionary, statutory code that stands in our way.
- Challenge unconstitutional laws targeted at the sector, especially those that infringe upon our First Amendment rights.
- Organize ourselves, our friends, and colleagues.

Some have argued, "I don't like the word *Defense*." When I was exploring titles for *Uncharitable*, some said, "You need a more positive title." But I didn't want a positive title; I wanted an honest one. In the book, I quoted Buckminster Fuller: "A problem well-stated is a problem well on its way to being solved." I wanted to state the problem clearly. And the title was designed for that purpose. It signaled that this is not just another book proposing bandages at the margins.

Similarly, our rights and our work need to be defended. That's the state of the problem right now. When that changes, we can change the description. But we must meet the issue where it's at, and this is where it's at.

Our system for creating change works against us. And it is axiomatic that if we do nothing to change that system, it will continue to work against us. We have the opportunity to eradicate the most hideous forms of human suffering in our lifetime. It is a possibility no generation before us has known. Hundreds of years ago, charity was about neighbor-to-neighbor assistance. We have a larger opportunity today. And the code for our ancestors' compassion will not suffice for our generation's dreams.

2

Build an Anti-Defamation League for Charity

[The Anti-Defamation League's] ultimate purpose is to secure justice and fair treatment to all citizens alike and to put an end forever to unjust and unfair discrimination against and ridicule of any sect or body of citizens.

ANTI-DEFAMATION LEAGUE CHARTER

In March 2010 the Boys and Girls Clubs of America, which receives federal funding support, came under attack by U.S. Senator Chuck Grassley (Republican of Iowa). He was making political red meat out of what he was characterizing as the excessive salary of the organization's CEO, Roxanne Spillett. But he did so out of context. The undeserved attack was then reported in a major segment on CNN, as well as in the *Washington Post*, the *Huffington Post*, *ABC News online*, and the Associated Press.

In his introduction to the piece, CNN's Wolf Blitzer commented, "This is a pretty shocking story," before he offered even one iota of information that would allow people to decide for themselves whether it was shocking.[1] He assured viewers that "this is going to cause a lot of consternation," thereby planting the seed of consternation while not reporting one conclusively consternating thing. All told, this reporting created what will likely now be a ten-year uphill public relations battle for the charity.

This will happen because the humanitarian sector had no dedicated agency there to prevent it. Its silence was deafening.

Voiceless

Blitzer introduced the Spillett story with swelling synthesizers playing in the background: "A CEO's million dollar salary . . . all of this is raising major eyebrows . . . we're talking about executives of the Boys & Girls Clubs."[2]

But there was no million-dollar salary. Spillett's base salary in 2008 was $360,774, plus a $150,000 bonus that the board had authorized based on her performance. She hadn't received a raise in the past two years. The rest of what made up the $988,591 she received that year consisted of $385,500 in "catch-up contributions for her underfunded retirement plan; and $9,165 for health benefits."[3] Moreover, the salary had been approved by the organization's national board, and an independent review had confirmed that the salary was in line with those of similar organizations.[4]

The issue here is not executive compensation. The story could just as easily have been about administrative overhead or something else. The issue is the consistently one-sided, negative reporting that is inflicted on the humanitarian sector—and the absence of an apparatus to prevent these stories from airing or, if they do, to ensure that sector leadership is included in the conversation. It isn't as if we wouldn't have had a response. It isn't as if we don't have a defense on the executive compensation issue or on any of the other issues that get used against us. Those defenses are compelling and could fundamentally alter the way the public thinks about the humanitarian sector.

In this case, there are indeed several "shocking" features to the story.

First, at no point did Blitzer, or his colleague, Lisa Sylvester, include in the segment the slightest cost-benefit analysis. How can you judge if a $510,744 salary and bonus are worth it if you don't inquire into what the person receiving the salary achieved? A first-year business school student would be kicked out of class for such egregious nonanalysis. In fact, in the past eight years under Spillett's leadership, the Boys & Girls Clubs tripled its network-wide revenues.[5] This is important because in 2008, the Boys & Girls Clubs had revenue of $1.5 billion. Suppose it had hired a lesser leader who required only $200,000 in compensation but didn't increase the organization's revenue at all? That would be a $310,000 savings in salary and a $1 billion loss in revenue. In one year! Under Spillett's leadership, the Boys & Girls Clubs also doubled the number of children served.[6] Wolf Blitzer didn't talk about that. There was no one during the newscast to challenge him to talk about it, so no one heard any of these facts. Had we as a sector been there, we would have had a response that would have put the public squarely on our side.

Senator Grassley didn't talk about any of these facts either—perhaps he didn't even know of them. He either purposely or unknowingly framed the issue as a zero-sum game. If he did it purposely, it's shameful; if he did it unknowingly, it's inexcusable incompetence on his part and on our sector's part for not making sure that he knew. "It appears that such [federal] funds are not reaching the intended beneficiaries, in this case, the youth of the country," Grassley and other senators said in a letter to the Boys & Girls Clubs.[7] But isn't the extra $1 billion a year in revenue produced under Spillett's leadership helpful to the youth of the country? Isn't doubling the number of kids served a sign that money is reaching the intended beneficiaries? And in any event, federal funds are not used to provide Spillett's compensation.[8] Nonetheless, Grassley accused the Boys & Girls Clubs, prior to any investigation, of "siphoning off" taxpayer money to high CEO salaries while some of the Boys & Girls Clubs are having to close because of the economy—as if the closures are a direct result of the CEO's compensation. A lot more clubs would have had to close if not for the extra revenue produced under Spillett's leadership. But under Grassley's logic and CNN's, the organization should go without a CEO and use the $510,000 to keep an extra one of its four thousand clubs open.

But this is not a zero-sum game. The money paid to a valuable CEO is not money taken away from the cause. It's an investment in the cause. How many clubs would have had to close if the organization had been without an effective CEO, or if it paid a person half as much and received only half as much productivity?

A rudimentary cost-benefit analysis would have noted that the Boys & Girls Clubs serves more than 4 million children and has a combined staff of fifty thousand full- and part-time employees. What does it take to effectively run an organization of that size? How do we attract and retain that competence?

But no one was there to ask these questions or to educate the public about the importance of asking these questions.

Double Standards

The second shocking aspect to the story is the cultural double standard that persists between the for-profit and the humanitarian sectors.

In 2008 the Walt Disney Company, which runs a sort of boys and girls club of its own, paid its CEO, Robert Iger, $51.1 million.[9] Steve Ballmer, CEO of Microsoft, manufacturer of the Xbox, which children use to play violent video games like "50 Cent: Blood on the Sand," and which comes with advisories warning of "blood," "drug reference," "intense violence," and "suggestive themes"—has a net worth estimated at $13.9 billion.[10] PepsiCo, which aggressively peddles its sugar water to kids, in 2008 paid its CEO, Indra Nooyi, $14.9 million.[11] Is the money paid to Robert Iger seen as denying kids more affordable access to Disneyland? Is Wolf Blitzer's salary, estimated in 2010 by Reuters to be $3 million,[12] framed as "siphoning" money from viewers? That people at the highest levels of government and the media are still looking at charity through this zero-sum lens is outrageous. But no one is there to point any of this out.

Consistent with this double standard the media claims that Senator Grassley is investigating the Boys & Girls Clubs because the organization received $41 million in government grants in 2008. By contrast, Lockheed Martin received 83 percent of its $45.2 billion 2009 revenues from U.S. government contracts.[13] Its CEO's 2010 compensation was $14.6 million—$111 million total over the last five years.[14] Neither CNN nor Senator Grassley inquired into that. No one was there to bring that up either.

The most shocking aspect of this story was that there was no independent national organization to defend the Boys & Girls Clubs—or to defend the executive compensation practices of the humanitarian sector in general—to offer an alternative point of view to the public or to rebut the arguments of Senator Grassley and CNN. The organization was left to fend for itself. Indeed, in the CNN story, it was not even there to defend itself or its practices.

As a result, the public hears only Wolf Blitzer's sensational and irrational conclusions, and it adopts the zero-sum thinking as its own. One YouTube comment on the story is, "This is very sad. I agree that a non-profit like this should be frugal and serve the people it's supposed to serve first. I agree with Senator Grassley on this one."[15] A commenter on ABC News wrote, "No way! . . . Anyone who goes to work for a nonprofit/charity goes into it knowing full well that it's not about the money. . . . To even consider accepting $1 million for such work is unacceptable and speaks volumes about this guy [*sic*] and his backwards thinking. The bulk of that money should be in the hands of the people who genuinely care for the boys and girls in need. This guy [*sic*] needs to be fired and whoever set and approved his salary should be fired as well."[16]

Even in the *Chronicle of Philanthropy*, the sector's own trade publication, readers railed against the Boys & Girls Clubs:

"No person working at a charity is worth paying more than $200,000 per year. That's just a simple fact. The people they hire should love the mission enough to not have a salary in such a huge range."[17]

"Here we go again! These runaway Non Profits with their exorbitant executive compensation and spending make me as sick as the For Profit organizations. Somebody needs to rein in this reckless get rich at all expenses mentality."[18]

"Yikes! . . . I cringe whenever a story like this surfaces. . . . [We are a] a grass-roots nonprofit that works on a shoestring budget. No salaries, no perks. Because we are small, we have control on spending. . . . I would hope that if we became as successful as the 'big guys,' we would still have the kind of ethics that would not allow out-of-control spending."[19]

Imagine if a thoughtful alternative voice had been there to simply state that a few hundred thousand dollars in extra annual investment had produced an extra billion dollars a year in revenue. The American people have common sense. Armed with that simple piece of information, they'd have come to a whole different conclusion. But they never had the chance.

The headline the public should have read was, "Brilliant Investment by Boys & Girls Clubs Reaps Massive Rewards for America's Youth." But there was no one to promote that headline.

Instead, the public got headlines like these: "Boys & Girls' Club CEO Roxanne Spillett's $1M Total Compensation Under Fire" (*ABC News*),[20] "Charity CEO Pay Questioned: Senators Want Answers Over Nonprofit Leader's $1 Million Compensation" (*Huffington Post*),[21] "Boys & Girls Clubs Outlook Clouded by National Dispute" (*Pittsburgh Tribune Review*),[22] and "Senators Question $1 Million Pay for Charity's CEO" (*Seattle Times*).[23]

Given these headlines, what do we expect the public to think?

I talked to an executive, who asked to remain anonymous, at a large regional Boys & Girls Club chapter after the story aired. This person called its effect "suffocating":

> Almost 80 percent of our donations come in restricted [now], and I am hearing especially from major donors . . . that they don't want anything, nothing [to go to administration and fundraising]; they want it restricted to programs and to kids. . . . They don't want to pay for staff. I have one donor [whose] annual gift is very, very generous, and she and her

> husband just say to me, "we won't pay for any staff. . . . I just want it to go directly to the kids." . . . [Donors] are also requesting more and more reports. . . . annual reports or quarterly reports. . . . on how the money was spent. . . . That affects our grant and development department because they are writing more reports, . . . which is administrative, which they won't pay for. Then our accounting office has to restrict the gifts. The auditors have to come in on an annual basis to make sure that we have restricted them properly and you know it is just a nightmare.[24]

It is no surprise that in June 2011, Roxanne Spillett announced her retirement as CEO of the Boys & Girls Clubs. *Youth Today* reported, "The board selected a successor from outside the national hierarchy, under which BGCA drew the ire of Congress. Spillett, the first woman to lead BGCA, has been a lightning rod for congressional criticism. . . . The boiling point came last year when four powerful Republican senators blocked what was to have been a $465 million special appropriation over five years to go to BGCA, questioning why Spillett received such a high salary."[25]

According to the newest "Daring to Lead" study, which surveys trends in humanitarian sector management, "About 2,000 of the roughly 3,000 executive directors of humanitarian organizations surveyed] expect to leave their jobs within five years. . . . Many of the leaders expressed concern that their boards are unfamiliar with the executive director's roles and responsibilities, and just one-third said they were very confident that their boards would hire the right successor."[26] This is probably because board members, like most of the general public, get their information from outlets like CNN.

This is also the price of our collective negligence. The effects of not responding to or actively preventing such reckless finger-pointing reach far beyond the Boys & Girls Clubs. These attacks bring down the image of the sector as a whole, reinforce the widely held public view that good organizations waste money, and make it harder to raise money.

This particular controversy was not limited to the issue of executive compensation. The Boys & Girls Clubs were also attacked, again without any cost-benefit analysis, for their spending on lobbying and travel. Blitzer opened his story by mentioning "millions spent on travel, conventions, lobbying fees." Is it automatically illegitimate for a $1.5 billion organization to spend millions on travel and lobbying? Shouldn't we examine the context of the expenditures?

The story raised suspicion about the $4 million that Boys & Girls Clubs had spent on travel.[27] The organization has four thousand clubs, so just one trip costing about one thousand dollars to each of them during the year would total $4 million. If you ask me, they should be spending more on travel.

But no one offered this argument. Had someone pointed it out, the public might have turned against CNN instead of the Boys & Girls Clubs.

The story also questioned the organization's spending $543,000 on lobbying. With appropriations like $465 million at stake, $543,000, which is 0.12 percent of $465 million, hardly seems excessive. To compare, in 2009, the U.S. Chamber of Commerce, which represents the interests of business, spent $145 million on lobbying. Exxon spent $27 million. Makers of pharmaceuticals and health products spent $267 million, "the most ever recorded by a single industry in a year," according to CBS News. Business associations spent $183 million.[28]

Yet we'd begrudge the Boys & Girls Clubs a tiny fraction of that spending to represent the interests of kids? Actually, we probably wouldn't. But no alternative voice was there to give the public the full story.

It is time to turn the moral tables and call this destructive sanctimony by its real name. Senator Grassley and CNN dealt a sucker punch to the Boys & Girls Clubs, its CEO, and the millions of kids it helps every day. But no one was there to call them on it.

If Martin Luther King Jr. had given Bull Connor the pass that the humanitarian sector gives to CNN, we'd still be waiting for a Voting Rights Act.

These Distortions Abound

Roxanne Spillett's story is not an isolated incident.

In May 2011, Long Island officials kicked off an investigation after the *New York Post* reported what it called the "outrageous" $363,205 salary ($244,132 in salary, $119,073 in other compensation) of Gail Barouh, CEO of the Long Island Association for AIDS Care.[29] The story began sarcastically: "Charity begins at home. . . . Barouh lives in a $1.4 million mansion in exclusive Cold Spring Harbor and drives a 2010 Mercedes-Benz to her charity's Hauppauge headquarters."[30] There were legitimate questions that should have been raised by the reporter but were not. For example, a house in Cold Spring Harbor that costs $1.4 million is not a mansion. Moreover, someone else could have been paying for all or part of the house, or the house may have been inherited. The reporter doesn't inquire. And does Mercedes know that charity leaders aren't supposed to buy their cars?

Again, executive compensation is not the issue here, or the merits of the arguments in favor of it being at certain levels—although those questions are important. Executive compensation just happens to be the issue the media most like to exploit because it sells the most media. The problem is the lack of a coordinated, collective, sector-wide response to state, local, and national issues reported by media that have sector-wide ramifications, including executive compensation.

A follow-up story in the *Post* reported Nassau County Comptroller George Maragos saying, prior to any investigation, that the salary was "out of line and inconsistent with [the organization's] mission to help people with AIDS who are in need of help." Following a guilty-until-proven-innocent principle, he ordered a "hold on all future contracts" with the organization.[31]

It's important to note that the organization's board co-chair said of the salary, "'We didn't pull something out of the air,' but went to a consulting firm that advised them how much to give her. . . . 'We need someone with experience. Dr. Barouh has that experience.'"[32]

Again, the zero-sum game analysis rears its head. Again, there was no cost-benefit analysis. Again, the leader of a charity was painted as demonic for earning the salary she did, even though corporate CEOs earn in a week what she does in a year. And again there was no independent national voice there to offer an alternative point of view to tell the public that the newspaper wasn't giving the full story.

Like the CNN story, this one doesn't end with the issue of executive salaries. The original *New York Post* article stated that the organization, which Barouh helped to found twenty-five years earlier, "spent 66 percent of its revenue on salaries that year," as if there's something wrong with that, and that "most of its charitable work involves running an AIDS hot line, which refers callers to other groups that provide medical and counseling services. . . . It also does some counseling and prevention services on its own." This is precisely the kind of charity work that requires a lot of salaried staff. But the public doesn't necessarily know that, and if no one tells them, they never will.

Nonetheless, the story continued, "Nassau Executive Edward Mangano . . . said he'll propose a bill requiring all county-funded nonprofits to spend at least 65 percent of their funds on charity—rather than on high salaries."[33]

This should have been challenged in the story. Or the challenge to it should have prevented it from running. Shouldn't the organization's own board determine what's high? And what if the people getting the salaries are providing the charity? In fact, the U.S. Supreme Court previously ruled that the types of requirements Mangano was proposing are not narrowly tailored to protect the public interest, precisely because charitable good can be embedded in things other than money that goes directly to those in need.[34] So the question is, What expertise does a Nassau executive have to be setting priorities for a charity, and why do we permit the press to hold him up as an expert?

Again, it's not about the issue of line staff salaries. It's about the lack of any coordinated, strategic effort to defend the organization, its staff, and the overall issue in the media.

A review of press releases from Mangano's office, as well as a review of all of Nassau County legislative meetings through August 2011, finds not a single reference to any newly imposed requirements on charities by Mangano. In fact, Mangano received a cease-and-desist letter in May 2011 from the charity's lawyers ordering him to stop the "dissemination of false information related to Dr. Barouh's compensation." The letter stated that the charity's board uses an "approved nationally r[illegible] management compensation survey" for determining [illegible] compensation and that Barouh's salary "falls within the [illegible]age for the scope and budget of the agency."[35]

This postmortem deserved its own story. The sector could have taken a huge victory lap that would have educated the public, but no one was there to pitch it.

In August 2011 the *New York Times* ran a story entitled, "Reaping Millions in Nonprofit Care for Disabled," about two brothers earning close to $1 million annually running a Medicaid-financed tax-exempt organization serving those with developmental disabilities.[36] The story raised legitimate concerns about the salaries, benefits, and practices of the two men. For sure, if there is anything illegal going on, the two should have the book thrown at them. But the story then listed the salaries of other executives not connected with the organization in question.

It took only a day for New York governor Andrew Cuomo to paint the entire New York charity community with the brush of suspicion raised by the story. He labeled the salaries reported in it as "startlingly excessive."[37] That's what happens when there's not a resource for the governor's office to call to coordinate with or when the sector doesn't have a tactical response.

The day after the story ran, the *New York Times* ran a follow-up, reporting, "Gov. Andrew M. Cuomo announced on Wednesday the creation of a task force to investigate executive compensation at nonprofit organizations that receive taxpayer subsidies from the state."[38] Cuomo said that these organizations have "a special obligation to the taxpayers that support them." He continued, "Executives at these not-for-profits should be using the taxpayer dollars they receive to help New Yorkers, not to line their own pockets." This is another case of a major political figure who doesn't hesitate to cast aspersions on the entire sector without any cost-benefit analysis and prior to any actual investigation. Why wouldn't he? He gains political popularity with zero negative political consequences.

Here was an opportunity to teach the general public about the ethical double standard we impose on the humanitarian sector. The governor seems to have had no intention of similarly investigating the salaries of for-profit executives whose companies receive state funding.

A review of New York State's contracts from January 2010 to March 2011 shows it awarded 22,994 contracts. Of those, about half, 9,279, went to nonprofit organizations. But in terms of money, during the same period the state awarded some $35.8 billion in contracts. Of that, only $3.2 billion, or 8.8 percent, went to nonprofit organizations. Ninety-one percent of the money, or $32.6 billion in taxpayer funds, went to contracts with companies and agencies that were not nonprofit.[39]

This fact is not what's important. It's that these kinds of facts exist but aren't part of the news story. It's that we keep taking punches to the face with our hands dangling lifeless at our sides.

Imagine if, in the context of the governor telling the public he wants an investigation because tax-exempt organizations receive state money, it were revealed to the public that 91 percent of all state contract money, totaling $32.6 billion, goes to for-profit or not nonprofit entities, and yet the governor was not looking to investigate those companies. Those executives are free to spend the public's money on whatever they want, from yachts and summer homes, to limousines, extravagant meals, jets, and everything else. Contemplating that might just change the public's view of the whole matter.

But here's what happens in the absence of those kinds of facts. The *Huffington Post* said outright, "The investigation will ensure that public money is going to help the intended recipients and is not being diverted to salaries."[40] The stories inspired impassioned comments like these:

"Fraud is Fraud and this practice has been going on for many years now. . . . How many of these big organizations are being run by their assistants? Many more than we all think."[41]

"Yes! It's important to know where the money you send in for donations goes. Hopefully not into some 'Leaders' pocket to pay for their Yacht."[42]

"This is why I for one have a problem with giving to charities you have no clue how much really goes to those in need. So I just cut out the middle man and give directly to the needy."[43]

"As a rule, I check the financials of any charity prior to donating. Specifically to weed out those that have unusually high 'administrative' expenses. The primary source is Charitynavi gator.org."[44]

"Congratulations Governor Cuomo. Let's see if you can carry it onto a national level, Possible President Cuomo. And that includes all the charities that have highly over paid executives that are constantly using the mantra; 'Donate-Donate-Donate.'"[45]

This is the price of our silence. The brushes tarring our organizations with labels of "fraud," "greed," and "excess" get hauled out and used again and again. That kind of repeated damage to the sector's integrity is what devastates public opinion.

But the consequences go even further. A few weeks later the *New York Times* reported that the governor's task force had sent an initial wave of letters to six hundred tax-exempt organizations that receive state funds, "demanding details about how much they pay their executives and board members." In an apparent presumption that charity executives commit perjury, the letters ask board members, rather than the executives themselves, to respond, because "executives are likely to have 'a significant interest in the size of their compensation.' " The letters gave organizations less than three weeks to respond and noted that "the regulatory agencies involved hold powerful leverage through their ability to cut off financing to groups that fail to comply."[46]

The letters then asked whether monies should be returned to the state and demanded to know the identity of the consultants each agency hired in determining compensation (as if boards have no capacity to determine compensation on their own) and whether the consultants "provided independent analysis or simply offered a justification for what the boards and executives already intended to do."[47]

Can we imagine a governmental authority ever doing this to a for-profit corporation that receives government funds? Of course not. The for-profit sector would never stand for it.

This time the public outcries were worse:

"Yes! Volunteers have often been collecting money in door-to-door campaigns just to end up funneling that money into the pockets of the non-profit executives. . . . This must stop."

"Most nonprofits' CEOs treat the organization as their own ATM. Can't wait to see the name and how much they have ripped off."

"For those of us who worked all our adult lives in non-profits, this move is welcome. And I would stress the idea of being on the lookout for extra sets of books lurking around, too."

"Sounds like Cuomo is 'ready to rumble.' Go get 'um, Andrew!"[48]

Ironically the salary information the governor is requesting is available in Form 990s, but apparently no one in government looked at them. The question people should be asking is what government leaders are doing to earn their pay. The governor, not the charities, should be on the defensive. We need a national voice asking the governor why his office never looked at the Form 990s of the organizations in question, or, if they did, why they never did anything about it until there was a *New York Times* story.

In another guilty-until-proven-innocent maneuver, the *Washington Post* ran this headline about Food & Friends, a major Washington, D.C., charity: "Montgomery County Strikes Back at D.C. Charity's Big Spending." Siding against the charity, the *Post* reporter wrote in the first sentence, "Montgomery County has registered its outrage over the huge salary paid to the chief of the Food & Friends charity." It further reported, "The county has stripped Food & Friends of a $55,000 earmark that helped the group serve meals to Montgomery residents. The move is a protest against the $357,000 in salary and benefits that the charity gives to its executive director."[49]

The pay of the leader in question is authorized every few years by the organization's board, which hires an independent consulting firm to advise it.[50] In the story, the firm is quoted as saying that the organization leader's compensation "falls between the 50th and 75th percentile of salaries in the competitive labor market and reflects [his] experience."[51]

Again without any cost-benefit analysis, and second-guessing the decision making of the organization's own board and consultants, the *Washington Post* concludes the story by saying, "This is a most welcome move by the MoCo [Montgomery County] council. Food & Friends by all accounts does much-needed work and does it well, but that's no excuse for running a charity as if it were a fancy for-profit business."[52]

The charity defended itself: "What we have here is the recommendation that 8,000 specialized meals and nutrition counseling will not be funded by the Montgomery County government on the strength of [council members'] personal objections to compensation determined after careful study by the board of directors of Food & Friends."[53]

But was anyone listening? Again, the sector let the county and the paper get away with it. There was no letter to the county from a national advocate demanding an apology. No alternative press strategy. No influx of e-mails from staff in the sector to put pressure on the paper and the county. Just the deer-in-the-headlights charity trying to defend itself.

The one-sided press has an effect. In a poll at the end of the story, 153 readers responded to the question, "Was Montgomery County right to strip Food & Friends of funding in protest over the salary of its executive director?" Eighty-six percent said yes.[54]

But the effect is even more profound than that, because political leaders are getting their education from the press too. The council member in question admitted that the decision to pull the funding was based on his "gut" intuition,[55] and, according to *Jewish Week*, he explained that "council members used solely their judgment, rather than a fiscal threshold." But he then admitted that "he neither referred to the group's 990 tax return nor developed a concrete method. . . . He did, however, look at 2008 *Washington Post* and *Washington Blade* articles examining pay rates at humanitarian organizations. 'No, I really didn't base the decision on a particular methodology,' Leventhal said. Food &

Friends 'has asked me the same question: "What is your precise methodology, what is your threshold?" . . . Well, this guy is making [around] $382,000. . . . That's too much! That's my test.' "[56]

The council member actually seems proud of his illiteracy on the subject. Again, there was no independent national voice there to express outrage or an alternative point of view.

In 2009 an Orlando, Florida, news reporter was stirring up controversy over charity CEO salaries. She asked Charity Navigator's CEO, Ken Berger, "Do you think these [nonprofit] CEOs deserve these big salaries?" Berger's response upheld the traditional point of view: "If you're talking about big, like $150,000—then I would say yes. If you're talking about half a million dollars, a million dollars, no! no. . . . If you want to make that kind of money there's something called the for-profit sector and you should feel free to go and work there."[57] That opinion was at odds with Charity Navigator's own Web site that at the time said, "We encourage you to look at CEO compensation as a percentage of total expenses. A charity CEO compensation of $200,000 for an organization spending $20 million per year (1%) probably seems much more reasonable than the same salary for a $1 million organization (20% of expenses for one person)."[58]

Someone should have been there to explore the ramifications of that view. Each of these one-sided stories is a teachable moment. Here's what we could have pointed out. In 2006 Gail McGovern, CEO of the American Red Cross, earned $565,000 against $3.4 billion in expenses or 0.02 percent of expenses. According to Ken Berger at the time, she should have gone into the for-profit sector and the Red Cross should have found someone to run its

$3 billion operation for around $150,000 per year. But according to the Charity Navigator Web site at the time, it would have been reasonable for her to be earning $34 million, or 1 percent of the organization's expenses.

Ironically, in 2009, the CEO of Charity Navigator earned $140,000 against expenses of $991,459.[59] That's 14.1 percent of expenses—seven hundred times more than the head of the Red Cross as a percentage of expenses. If the head of the Red Cross made 14 percent of expenses, her salary would be $476 million. The head of another watchdog (and frequent critic of high salaries in the sector), the American Institute of Philanthropy (AIP), earned $147,977 against just $463,704 in expenses in 2010, or 31.9 percent.[60] If each were paid 1 percent of expenses, as the Charity Navigator site suggested was reasonable, their salaries should have been $10,000 and $4,600, respectively.

None of these inconsistencies was brought to light. And it's those traditional sources—Charity Navigator and AIP—that the media consult to reinforce their biases. Daniel Borochoff of AIP was quoted in the *Washington Post* as stating that the salary of the head of Food & Friends "appears excessive in relation to other nonprofits in related fields."[61] The salary was 4.6 percent of the organization's expenses.[62] Borochoff's salary, by contrast, was 28 percent of his organization's expenses.

But the public didn't learn this. We didn't tell them.

To Ken Berger's great credit, he co-issued a press release in 2009, along with other charity evaluators, stating that "overhead ratios and executive salaries are useless for evaluating a nonprofit's impact." But the sector wasn't there to spread this news.

Why did the sector not come to the aid of any of these organizations or to the defense of the issues raised in these instances? Because it has no organization chartered specifically to do that.

Other Communities Stand Up for Themselves

The American Jewish community has the Anti-Defamation League. The gay community has GLAAD—the Gay and Lesbian Alliance Against Defamation. The African American community has the NAACP to respond to disparagement and to work to prevent it. But the humanitarian sector has no corollary—no organization chartered specifically to address and correct sensational media attacks on the sector or its members. It has no organization chartered specifically to train the media on the realities of humanitarian sector business practice, to bust myths and correct misunderstandings. It has no characters on television shows to enlighten the public about what it's like to work in the sector. As a result, outrageous media attacks go unaddressed, and the public is left to believe exactly what the media tell it.

What's ironic is that the Anti-Defamation League, GLAAD, the NAACP, and other organizations like them are all charitable organizations. So while they defend attacks against Jews, gays and lesbians, African Americans, and others, there's no one to respond to attacks against the anti-defamation organizations themselves. No one defends the defenders.

A visit to the GLAAD Web site features a scrolling list of actions and calls to action: "Demand the *Batesville Daily Guard* Show Respect to Grieving Partner," "[Actor] Tracy Morgan Meets with LGBT [(Lesbian, Gay, Bi-Sexual, Transgender)] Advocates and Publicly Apologizes in Nashville," "Demand That the Media Report Killings of LGBT Puerto Ricans," and "GLAAD Hosts National People of Color Media Institute."[63]

This is a community in committed action. It's professionalized activism, born of a deep, unapologetic, uncompromising regard for the community's right to exist. GLAAD is determined to turn the tide of history by methodically reshaping the media's reporting on the community. The contrast with the humanitarian sector's self-esteem and self-defense could not be starker.

GLAAD has been at it for twenty-five years. It was formed in 1985 in protest of "defamatory and sensationalized" reporting on the AIDS epidemic by the *New York Post*.[64] GLAAD describes itself as "the leading organization that works directly with the news, entertainment, and social media to ensure that our stories are heard—because as people get to know the LGBT community they come to understand that we simply seek and deserve the same things all Americans do."[65] GLAAD states that it is "a story-teller, watchdog, and advocate—empowering real people to share their stories, holding the media accountable for the words and images they present, and helping grassroots organizations communicate effectively."[66]

The organization has a tightly honed, sophisticated approach. It has developed relationships with media insiders and has a highly developed media field program that focuses on rural communities and trains people to speak up for themselves and use social media.

GLAAD summarizes its perspective in this way: "We believe that people are fair, and when they see LGBT people, when they hear our stories, they will come to understand that this is about people just like them—their brothers and sisters, neighbors and friends—who deserve to be accepted, respected, and valued."[67] Change a few of those words, and we have the mission for an anti-defamation league for the humanitarian sector: "We believe that people are fair, and when they see the reality of what people in the sector do, and understand the reality of what it really costs to solve entrenched social problems, they will come to understand that we are all fighting for the same thing, and that people working in the sector deserve to be respected and valued."

GLAAD's work has had an effect. Consider the progress that the gay and lesbian community has made on its issues over the past two decades. Public opinion on gay marriage shifted from 11 percent in favor in 1985 to 53 percent in favor in 2011.[68] It is now legal in seven states and the District of Columbia to issue marriage licenses to same-sex couples. What used to be an issue that politicians sought to avoid like the plague for fear of alienating the middle has now made people like Andrew Cuomo the darlings of the party. Public opinion on gays and lesbians in the military has shifted from 51 percent in favor in the late 1970s to 70 percent in favor now.[69] In December 2010, President Obama signed a law deauthorizing the don't ask/don't tell policy, and gays and lesbians can now proudly serve in the military.

These changes in public opinion are the result of both action and expenditure. GLAAD has a $6.5 million annual budget.[70] Over the course of its twenty-five-year history it has spent many tens of millions of dollars doing this work.

Our sector does have an extremely proficient and hard-working national advocacy organization: Independent Sector. It has an annual budget of about $8 million.[71] Its mission is to "advance the common good by leading, strengthening, and mobilizing the nonprofit and philanthropic community."[72] It focuses on public policy, nonprofit effectiveness, accountability, and networking, not on media. It is not chartered to transform the media's relationship to the sector.

This organization, again, which is not chartered to tackle media, is the only major advocate for community-based humanitarian service providers. The gay and lesbian community, by contrast, has several advocacy organizations in addition to GLAAD:

- The Human Rights Campaign mobilizes the grassroots with a million members. Its 2009 budget was $25 million.[73]
- The National Gay & Lesbian Task Force, which also mobilizes the grassroots, has a $7.6 million annual budget.[74]
- Lambda Legal, which litigates, advocates, and educates, has a $15.6 million annual budget.[75]
- PFLAG—Parents, Families, and Friends of Lesbians and Gays educates the public and has a $2.7 million annual budget.[76]

In addition, many other local organizations are working on raising public consciousness about these issues. That's more than $60 million every year going into changing public attitudes about the gay and lesbian community.

The Jewish Anti-Defamation League has a $70 million annual budget.[77] The NAACP has an annual budget of $28.4 million.[78] By contrast, the humanitarian sector puts effectively no collective strategic resources into shaping media and public opinion about itself.

It's not as if the humanitarian sector is small compared to these other communities. The sector has some 13 to 15 million employees.[79] That's about 10 percent of the 153 million people in the U.S. workforce overall.[80] And it's not as if the stakes are of less import. The stakes could not be higher.

The problem is more fundamental than that the sector lacks a resource to respond methodically to inaccurate media stories or to educate and interact with media. We lack an understanding of where we'd begin. We lack research and data on the subject. We have no resource to tell us, for example, how many stories the media released on charities in the past year. What percentage were positive? What percentage were inaccurate? What are the most repeated inaccuracies? What are the most common misperceptions? What data do the media want from the sector? What missing information or data frustrates them the most?

More than one reporter I spoke to on the subject told me that if we really want to reach the media, we should be doing presentations and tracks at the Investigative Reporters and Editors Conference, the Radio Television Digital News Association Conference, or the annual conference of the Society of Professional Journalists. My guess is that few charity executive directors, or maybe even none of them, has even heard of these organizations. We mingle with ourselves in a bubble that consists of a hundred different nonprofit sector gatherings, preaching to our own choirs about what ails us.

But I believe we can change minds. At my talks, there are always a few laypeople who arrive with all of the traditional prejudices about charity that our culture has instilled in them. But after my forty-five-minute presentation on the flaws in overhead ratios, for example, they come up to me and say something like: "I am never going to ask that question about what percentage of my donation goes to the cause again." One reliable control group for evaluating the effect of a little dose of information is the audiovisual technicians in the room. They are always there, and since they are running the sound board or the video camera, they have to listen. They often come up to me after a talk and say, "You know, I never thought about these things before. What you say makes a lot of sense." It's likely the first time anyone has ever invited them to think about the subject, and it takes only a little thought to change a mind. I believe we can achieve similar results with the media.

For example, a reporter from *NBC News* in Kansas City called me in 2011. He was doing a story based on a *Fortune* magazine list he had seen of the one hundred best charities in America. He wanted to compile a similar list for Kansas City and planned to base the list on the only data that were readily available: overhead ratios. I gave him all the reasons I believed that was a very bad idea. When I interviewed him for this book months later, it turned out that he never ran the story. He gave this explanation: "Well, I went to you for clarity. After my conversation with you, I was more confused than I was before I Googled your name. So, yeah, the conversation I had with you was the final nail in the coffin of that story."[81] He said that prior to our discussion, his default method for evaluating a charity would have been "the administrative overhead compared to the amount of money they were taking in compared to what ultimately went to the charitable intent."

Reporters typically go to the same tired wells to source their stories and inform their own views. Even among sophisticated reporters, overhead ratios and executive compensation play a huge role in determining support. One reporter I spoke to said he personally gives to a local charity in Pittsburgh based on those factors:

> They have the lowest expense of just about any foundation or nonprofit you can imagine; they get the highest ratings in Charity Navigator—I know the executive compensation for their CEO and for an organization of its size. . . . He doesn't make anywhere near as much money as other CEOs make—everything goes to helping people around the world, and I really respect the work they do so that's why I like to support them. [The ratio of expenses to revenues has] got to be under 1 percent for that group.[82]

Here's what some others said about getting information about charities:

"I would immediately go to the Better Business Bureau and I would go to GuideStar."[83]

"Typically when I'm reporting on nonprofit issues I try to start with the 990 that I get from GuideStar."[84]

"[When people ask me how to research a charity, I tell them] look at what they do. . . . Then go check out their financial filings . . . on GuideStar . . . and then sometimes I point people to Charity Navigator."[85]

But a reporter for the *Boston Globe* reflected on how her reporting approach has evolved from the norm as a result of a more sophisticated understanding of humanitarian sector business practice, gained from years of reporting on the sector:

> I may come to it from a slightly different view. . . . Some things that might seem like a big deal to other reporters don't necessarily seem like a big deal to me. A little bit of a high salary is not going to be as interesting to me as conflicts of interest or self dealing or boards doing a bad job.[86]

Clearly a little bit of education makes a big difference.

I spoke to a few of the reporters who have interviewed me for various stories on different charities over the past year. Here's what they had to say about the way they report, the state of media reporting on the sector, and the need for improvement:

On Access to Resources

"I think it is up to the charities to . . . [say] here are some experts that you should turn to."[87]

"We are even seeing it in Congress . . . government getting more aggressive with [nonprofits]—and I think that has a lot to do with the fact that there is no . . . advocacy group—they don't really speak with one voice—they all sort of hide."[88]

"For the foundations that have hundreds of billions of dollars in assets and yet they don't put out any . . . [communications]. . . . They're not there—they are easy targets for government because government leaders know they don't defend themselves."[89]

"[I would grade the sector as] pretty poor [at defending itself]."[90]

On How Much Humanitarian Organizations Should Get Better at Talking to the Public About the Need to Fund Overhead

"Oh. Way better. Way better."[91]

There are exciting opportunities to turn around public opinion for the sector. We simply have to dedicate ourselves to them, and that's exactly what the Charity Defense Council will do.

Next Steps

We have to build an anti-defamation apparatus every bit as powerful as those created by other communities. It must be well funded, capable, strategic, and tactical. It must have as its goal a 180-degree turnaround, in short order, in the nature of media reporting on the humanitarian sector. Within the first year, people should sense a difference in the national media posture toward our sector. Our commitment to this initiative and to our own must be unwavering.

First, we need baseline research on the current lay of the media land. Who are the sector's friends in the media? Who are its media enemies right now? What are the most common reporting mistakes? What are the greatest myths we need to confront?

We can't develop a game plan until we understand whom we're playing against and what game they're playing. And we can't measure the progress we're making until we know what the baseline was from which we began.

Next, we must let the media know that a new voice and a new resource with a strong and particular point of view has arisen, that we are available as a resource, and that we intend to be heard. We will create separate units to liaise with the media across their own categories: national magazine, national news broadcast, national talk broadcast, major metropolitan print, national digital news, the blogosphere, local broadcast news, and local magazine and print. We will become experts in understanding the players in these fields, and we will create productive relationships with them.

In addition, we must rally the support of the entire sector and organize it to address media issues specifically. If we are well organized, we can unleash a chorus of national voices on reporters in advance of stories that we know are going to run, and comment on stories after they run so that there is no longer an imbalance of comments against the sector but a majority in its favor. We can influence stories before they go to print and stop malicious stories from being run in the first place; write opinion pieces about media coverage and important public policy issues being debated in the media; and make ourselves available for on-air interviews, call-ins, and comments on Internet, radio, and television programs that cover important sector issues.

We must educate the media on our point of view with regular outbound communications, story ideas based on successful models, innovations and results that humanitarian organizations are producing every day, and local workshops. If the media have inspiring stories about innovations going on in the sector, they won't have to use scandal as the only angle to report on the sector. It's our responsibility to provide the media with those stories. In this age of slashed investigative news budgets, the media lack the resources to seek out those stories on their own.

We must become a major presence at the conferences at which investigative reporters and other media gather. We must have our own booths, keynote speakers in the programs, and workshops dedicated to the sector, and they must become a mainstay of each conference's menu of break-out sessions. All of these initiatives will establish an important presence for us that will reap rewards immediately and down the road.

We must develop our own media and content division that conceives, secures funding for, and creates documentaries and educational programming—provocative, stimulating, and compelling *Inconvenient Truth*–style educational content—for broadcast by the major media and for donor and constituent education.

In summary, the media need a powerful, respected, and legitimate resource other than the watchdogs. The public needs to hear an alternative point of view. Wolf Blitzer and his colleagues have to understand that they cannot with impunity get ratings by taking potshots at major charities doing important work. Political figures need to realize that too. We need a new era of public and media celebration of the humanitarian sector's successes and value. This is what we intend to create.

3

Create a "Got Milk?" Campaign for Charity

The enemies of advertising are the enemies of freedom.

J. ENOCH POWELL

There are two types of media: nonpaid and paid. Nonpaid media—news stories—were the subject of the previous chapter. These stories can be positive, like one about the newest iPad, or negative, like some of the stories related in Chapter Two. It's free publicity, whether you like it or not. Because you don't pay for it, you don't control the message. Paid media are what we all refer to as advertising: television ads, billboards, radio ads, banner ads on Web sites, magazine ads, and so on. You have complete control over the message, down to the pixel. That's why you pay.

Whether you're a person, a soda brand, or an entire sector, your reputation in the media is the net effect of how you come across in paid and nonpaid media. So, for example, when Toyotas began crashing into things because of allegedly faulty braking systems a couple of years ago (Toyota was later exonerated on the braking issue by the U.S. Department of Transportation), Toyota got billions of dollars in negative nonpaid media.[1] It tried to offset that with millions of dollars in paid media, mostly in the form of full-page ads explaining its side of the story and what it was doing to correct the problem.

That you want to minimize your negative nonpaid media goes without saying. You try to offset the effects of negative nonpaid media with paid media, telling your side of the story. If you get a lot of negative nonpaid media, the last thing you want to do is leave it out there, unaddressed, with zero paid media telling your side of the story.

That's exactly what the humanitarian sector does.

Our sector gets a lot of negative nonpaid media. It doesn't do anything to try to influence that, as we saw in the previous chapter. It then makes matters worse by spending nothing on paid media to offset it.

Reputation in the media is only one part of overall reputation. How big a part depends on what else you do to build your brand. Apple's reputation, for example, is created first and foremost by the products it makes. If people love their iPads and tell their friends how much they love their iPads, a reporter who writes a cynical review of the device might not have much of an impact. Conversely, if people were extremely dissatisfied with the performance of the device, it wouldn't matter much if Apple bought tons of advertising telling people the device was great. Word would get around that it isn't.

Apple has other weapons in its arsenal for creating its reputation. It has its retail stores and the quality of those stores and their customer service, its tech support, and its leaders. Its reputation in the media is only one part, and probably not the most important part, of its overall reputation. The quality of its products alone vastly outweighs its reputation in the media.

Individual charities are a little like Apple. They too have a lot of weapons in their reputation-building arsenal: board members with connections in the community, staff members who have solid relationships with donors and volunteers, and walk-a-thons and gala dinners at which they get to talk about their brands.

The humanitarian sector as a whole, however, doesn't have those weapons. It doesn't have a building. It doesn't have a board. It doesn't have a walk-a-thon. The sector is an abstraction to most people.

So the overall reputation of the humanitarian sector is extremely dependent, if not wholly dependent, on its reputation in the media. But its current reputation in the media consists of a lot of negative nonpaid media, which the sector doesn't attempt to influence, and zero paid media to offset the effects of all of the negative nonpaid media.

That's a perfect storm of negativity.

We can change this by investing in smart paid media. That's what this chapter is about.

The Nature of Zero

Imagine if you were deaf in one ear but never told anyone. Yet you wondered why people always tried speaking to you in the inoperative ear; you got frustrated that they didn't recognize your condition; and you got angry at them because they kept doing it over and over. The humanitarian sector is like that.

The sector has never engaged the public in a conversation about itself and its issues. We lament the fact that the public demands low overhead, even though spending on the things labeled "overhead" is what our sector needs to make progress. But we have never spent any money on advertising to tell the public this. We bemoan the fact that the public goes into a rage when they see relatively high executive compensation, even though we need higher levels of leadership compensation to ntivize the world's best talent. But we have never advertising to make this case. We despair that ublic will never understand the realities of our work, yet we have never once spoken to them, as a whole, as a sector, in the medium of paid advertising in the way that business does about those realities.

We have not told the public that overhead ratios don't reveal anything about the quality of the programs at the charities they support. So they continue to think the overhead ratios matter. We have not told the public that the sector must advertise in order to build market demand for charity and that investments in advertising can multiply the impact of a donor's gift. So the public thinks that charity spending on advertising is wasteful. We consistently fail to tell the public about all of the incredible results the sector as a whole achieves every day. So the public continues to think that we waste their money.

It would be bad enough if we were simply remaining silent on these matters. But it's worse than that: we have been actively contaminating the public's thinking about these issues by reinforcing the mistaken beliefs they already hold. We actually engage in a form of paid media that works against us. We put large pie charts on our Web sites (which we pay to build) showing donors how little we spend on overhead, reassuring the public that low overhead is our top priority. We place the watchdog seals of approval—at least one of which you have to pay to acquire and which have traditionally required meeting certain low overhead and low executive compensation thresholds—in prominent places on our Web sites and in our press materials.

In other words, we don't just sanction the public's misguided prejudices; we nurture them. Then we wonder why the public is misguided.

The time has come to speak up, collectively, proactively, and strategically, on behalf of ourselves, our organizations, our donors, and, most of all, those we serve.

What would we have to spend on a campaign to make a difference: $5 million a year? $10 million? How would we get it? Donated advertising is always the default plan in our sector. In many circles, it wouldn't even occur to people to think of it in any other way: "If we can't get it donated, we can't do it at all." That's the reality we are taught to live in, and we wouldn't think of violating it. Imagine if we told Apple that the only way it could advertise the iPad is if it got the ads donated, according to someone else's whims, based on the availability of hand-me-down, cancelled ad space, instead of an integrated plan Apple had thoughtfully developed on its own to produce results.

Before we look at what money we should spend, I want to reflect briefly on what it means to have spent not a penny—not on a single newspaper ad, a billboard, or a TV ad—to enlighten people about our issues. I want to reflect on the existential nature of zero.

But let's start with a number considerably higher than zero. Let's start with $3,318,960. Imagine a humanitarian organization spending $3.3 million to advertise its cause. In a "nonprofit" context, this sounds like an enormous amount of money. We can hear critics calling it an abomination for a humanitarian organization to spend millions promoting itself when that $3.3 million could have gone to the needy. *Shame on the organization*, they say.

$3,318,960 is the amount of money that Save the Children, one of the largest international development and relief organizations in the world, spent on advertising in 2009.[2]

In contrast, the Walt Disney Company spent $1,931,700,000 on advertising in 2010—582 times more than what Save the Children spent on advertising the year before.[3] That's a factor equivalent to the difference between the height of a ten-month-old infant and the Sears Tower. Picture that in your mind for a moment: the baby, seated, in a diaper, on the sidewalk, looking way, way, way up to the very top of the Sears Tower. Save the Children: 1; Entertain the Children: 582.

Here's how Disney's 2010 ad spending breaks down. It spent $178 million on magazine ads, $87 million on newspaper ads, $36 million on billboards, $58 million on radio ads, $187 million on Internet ads, and $546 million—over half a billion dollars—on television ads. Disney spent an additional $838 million on what is called "unmeasured" media—for example, promotional events, direct mail, and coupons: $838 million!

The iconic liberal economist John Kenneth Galbraith lamented the massive difference in resources our society puts into promoting the consumption of private goods—like entertainment—and promoting public goods—like saving children. This is his worst fear writ large.

In 2009 Save the Children had total expenses of $465,047,995.[4] So the money it spent on advertising represented just 0.713 percent of its total expenditures. In 2010 Disney had $31.3 billion in expenses.[5] So its advertising was 6.1 percent of its expenses—nine times more as a percentage of the organization's expenses than Save the Children's. This ratio suggests that Disney values the recruitment of new "buyers" (or donors, to translate) nine times more than Save the Children does. And Save the Children spends more on advertising as a percentage of its expenses than the typical health and human services charity.

Figure 3.1 shows how some of the most popular charities in America, working on some of the most urgent causes of our time, compare with issue-related consumer brands, selling nonessential discretionary goods and services, on their advertising spending.

Compared to the money that consumer brands spend on advertising, the amounts individual charities spend are negligible on both a dollar basis and as a percentage of the organizations' expenses. If the $3.3 million that Save the Children spent on advertising and the $18.5 million that Susan G. Komen spent on advertising amounts to virtually nothing, then what is the $0.00 that the humanitarian sector spends collectively to educate the public about sector-wide issues? It begins to approach the nature of a negative. The symbolism is powerful.

Zero is what the humanitarian sector as a whole spends on its collective effort to educate the public about fundamental issues that stand in the way of our ability to make progress. We have no mechanism for coming together to speak to the public as one on behalf of all.

None of this would be of any moment if advertising didn't make a difference. But it's unfathomable that year after year, Disney, Anheuser-Busch, Mars, L'Oréal, and all the other consumer product companies would spend billions of dollars on advertising—dollars that could otherwise go directly to bottom-line profit—if it didn't help sales and build demand for their offerings.

Gigantic consumer brands are creating new wants and desires for all manner of new products—putting all kinds of new ideas in the consumer's mind about flat screen televisions and luxury cruises and lipstick. Yet the number of new ideas the humanitarian sector has tried to implant in the public's mind—about our sector, its achievements, and new ways we might change the world together—amounts to precisely zero.

Other industries join together. Milk producers have organized together to bring to the public a unified message about the benefits of drinking milk. Similar efforts have been launched by

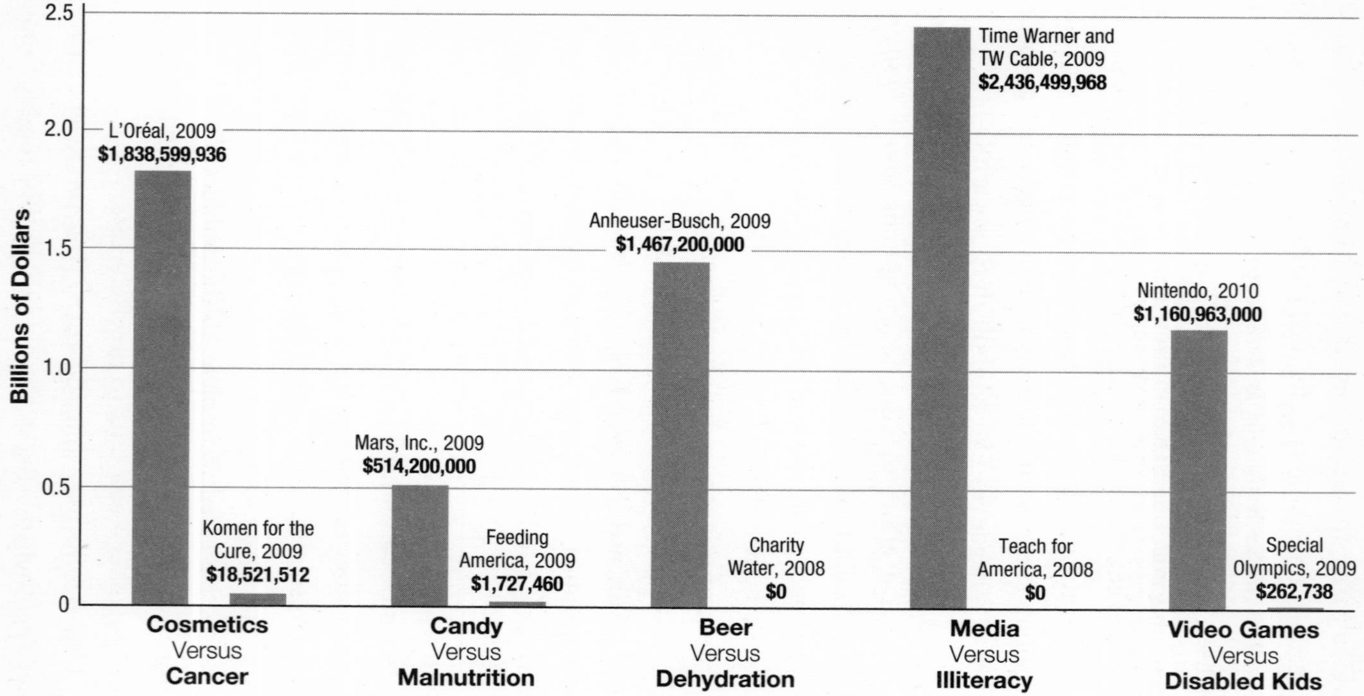

Billions of Dollars
2.5
2.0
1.5
1.0
0.5
0
L'Oréal, 2009
$1,838,599,936
Komen for the Cure, 2009
$18,521,512
Cosmetics Versus Cancer
Mars, Inc., 2009
$514,200,000
Feeding America, 2009
$1,727,460
Candy Versus Malnutrition
Anheuser-Busch, 2009
$1,467,200,000
Charity Water, 2008
$0
Beer Versus Dehydration
Time Warner and TW Cable, 2009
$2,436,499,968
Teach for America, 2008
$0
Media Versus Illiteracy
Nintendo, 2010
$1,160,963,000
Special Olympics, 2009
$262,738
Video Games Versus Disabled Kids

Figure 3.1 Charity Versus Consumer Brand Advertising by Issue

Sources: Advertising Age. Department of the Treasury, Internal Revenue Service, "Form 990: Return of Organization Exempt from Income Tax," filing organization: Susan G Komen Cancer FDN Inc, Dallas, TX, filing year: 2009, http://www.guidestar.org/FinDocuments//2010/751/835/2010–751835298–06abb833–9.pdf. Advertising Age. U.S. Department of the Treasury, Internal Revenue Service, "Form 990: Return of Organization Exempt from Income Tax," filing organization: Feeding America, Chicago, filing year: 2009, http://www.guidestar.org/FinDocuments//2010/363/673/2010–363673599–06af4916–9.pdf. Advertising Age. U.S. Department of the Treasury, Internal Revenue Service, "Form 990: Return of Organization Exempt from Income Tax," filing organization: Charity Global, New York, filing year: 2008, http://www.aidforafrica.org/wp-content/uploads/2010/07/charity-water-990.pdf. Advertising Age. Department of the Treasury, Internal Revenue Service, "Form 990: Return of Organization Exempt from Income Tax," filing organization: Teach for America, New York, filing year: 2009, http://www.guidestar.org/FinDocuments//2009/133/541/2009–133541913–063a4a9a-9A.pdf. Nintendo, *2011 Annual Report*, http://www.nintendo.co.jp/ir/pdf/2011/annual1103e.pdf, accessed Feb. 2012. U.S. Department of the Treasury, Internal Revenue Service, "Form 990: Return of Organization Exempt from Income Tax," filing organization: Special Olympics Inc., Washington, DC, filing year: 2009, http://www.guidestar.org/FinDocuments//2009/520/889/2009–520889518–065f3f7f-9.pdf.

the oil industry, the plastics industry, and orange juice, cotton, and egg producers.

"The Incredible, Edible Egg"

When egg producers decided that they needed to sell more eggs in the late 1970s, they realized they needed to change the image of the egg, which at the time most people thought of as an unhealthy, high-cholesterol heart attack waiting to happen. The producers understood that they would have strength in numbers —that one egg farmer wasn't going to be able to change the way Americans thought about eggs and that a hundred egg farmers, each spending a little bit of money on a hundred different messages, would at best confuse the public. So they came together as one and created a single, memorable, unified message. They pooled their money in order to convey their single message to the public using advertising.

The result was "the incredible, edible egg" campaign, which has now been running for three decades.[6] It's managed by the American Egg Board (AEB). Yes, there is an American Egg Board. Its Web site announces that it is "U.S. egg producer's link to consumers in communicating the value of the incredible egg. Our mission is to increase demand for egg and egg products on behalf of U.S. egg producers."[7] The Web site trumpets, "Want to be incredible? Eat incredible!"[8] and showcases commercials touting the benefits of eating eggs. They even try to get you to get your kids to eat more eggs. One commercial shows a dad rehearsing a school play with his son. The man appears in drag wearing a princess's wig and reciting his lines in falsetto at his son's request. The narrator says, "You do everything so they're at their best. So start their big days with the incredible protein. Eggs!"[9] A text box pops up that says, "Only 15 cents!" The ads were running on *Good Morning America*, the *Rachael Ray Show*, the Food Network, and online in August 2011.

In 2009 the AEB spent $15,843,665 on advertising and marketing—63 percent of its program expenditures.[10] That's about $15.8 million more than the humanitarian sector spent advocating on its own behalf. That money would buy the sector, at a minimum, one full-page ad, and possibly two, in each of the ten largest metropolitan U.S. newspapers, every single month, for an entire year.

That would be a nice start.

This sort of advertising spending seems to work. The AEB 2010 annual report stated, "In the past year, egg-related products available for breakfast at quick-service restaurants (QSRs) increased by an incredible 47 million servings."

The AEB also focuses on other forms of advertising like outreach. For example, it reported that it had been working for years with Subway on its breakfast program, which ultimately resulted "in the introduction of a national breakfast program in April 2010 at 24,000 locations."[11] Imagine if the humanitarian sector did similar outreach with media, high schools, colleges, or, for that matter, Subway.

The AEB is also a savvy social media player. In 2010 it reported:

> The incredible edible egg appeared on Facebook, Twitter, YouTube, Flickr, and IncredibleEgg.org, resulting in billions of impressions annually. . . . Online communications and engagement promoted the value of eggs and highlighted quick-and-easy egg recipes, news about eggs . . . on websites such as Weightwatchers, Yahoo, AllRecipes, Scholastic, About, Hulu, Blogher, and WildTangent. Ad word programming with Google and Bing ensured that AEB content appears high in egg-related searches. AEB increased engagement with fans on The Incredible Edible Egg Facebook page through weekly polls about eggs. The page also encouraged fans to post their own recipes and photos, comment on twice-weekly recipe posts, and read status updates regarding interesting egg facts.[12]

As of 2011, the Egg Board's Facebook page had 130,000 likes.[13] For eggs! By contrast, the Facebook page of Independent

Sector, the charitable sector's largest advocacy group, had 1,047 likes—for an industry that employs 10 million Americans.

Can it really be that Americans like eggs 130 times more than they like helping others? Of course not. These are simply the effects of advertising, or rather, of not advertising.

"Pork, the Other White Meat"

In 1987, pork producers decided that in order to sell more pork, they had to change the image of pork as a fatty, unhealthy meat. Like the egg farmers, they decided that no one pig farmer was going to be able to change the way Americans think about pork. So like the egg farmers, they joined forces, pooled their money, and made a big paid-media splash.

The National Pork Board (NPB) began an "aggressive media campaign directed at U.S. consumers" designed to "increase consumer demand for pork and to dispel pork's reputation as a fatty protein."[14] The campaign's slogan was, "Pork, the other white meat." The NPB reports that a 2000 study by Northwestern University found "the Other White Meat brand to be the fifth most memorable promotional tagline in the history of contemporary advertising."[15] A 1997 U.S. Department of Agriculture report noted that "research indicates that consumers now are less likely to perceive pork negatively in terms of fat, calories, and cholesterol than before the advertising began."[16]

In 1991 the *New York Times* reported that as a result of the "costly and intensive campaign," sales of pork rose by 20 percent, from $25 billion to $30 billion.[17]

If we can change the way the public thinks about pork, we can change the way it thinks about charity. And if U.S. charitable contributions grew by 20 percent over the course of five years, it would increase giving by $60 billion a year—an amount greater than all annual foundation giving in America combined.[18] Sixty billion dollars is more than one and a half times all giving to international causes. Now we're talking scale.[19]

Pork's slogan in 2011 was, "Pork, be inspired."[20] By pork?! They've stolen our message! What people should be getting inspired by is the difference the humanitarian sector makes in the lives of millions of human beings every day and how many more lives it could help with more resources.

The Pork Board's Facebook page has seventeen thousand likes.[21]

Do You Own an Oil Company?

In 2008, in the face of high gasoline prices, the oil industry upped its ad spending by 17 percent over the prior year, to $53 million per quarter. National Public Radio reported that in April of that year, the American Petroleum Institute (API) launched an ad campaign with this question: "Do you own an oil company?" It then cited "a commissioned study showing that 41 percent of oil company stocks are held by investors in mutual funds, pensions or 'other investments' "and that "API spent $3.8 million during the first quarter" of the year alone on just that campaign. The advertising seems to have worked. API president Red Cavaney quoted a Gallup poll showing a 14 percent drop in the number of Americans blaming oil companies for higher gas prices in just one year.[22]

If we can change the way the public thinks about the oil industry, we can change the way it thinks about charity.

The API Web site shows twelve different television ads, seven different radio ads, and twenty-four different full-page newspaper ads it has recently run.[23] In 2010 API spent more than $39 million on advertising for the industry.[24]

The American Petroleum Institute's Facebook page has 10,866 likes, ten times more than the humanitarian sector's advocacy organization.[25]

"Got Milk?"

"Got Milk?" is probably the most famous ad campaign ever run on behalf of a single industry.

In the early 1990s, milk consumption in California was down a worrisome 20 percent over 1980, and the industry was facing increasing competition from a variety of sodas, juices, bottled waters, sports drinks, and other nondairy beverages, as well as from people eating out more often.[26] Like the small egg and pork producers, California milk bottlers decided they needed to band together to confront this reality. According to Jeff Manning, head of the California Milk Processor Board (CMPB), in 1993 California milk processors "decided to take charge of their own marketing destiny . . . create great advertising and sell more milk."[27]

The "Got Milk?" campaign was born.

The creative brief, a tool that ad agencies use to guide messages, was simple: "Milk sales are going down. We need them to go up. Get people to consume more milk when they're at home and buy more milk . . . when they're at the store. . . . Change beliefs and attitudes."[28] The campaign purposely circumvented those who were not big milk fans to begin with and instead targeted those who already drank milk frequently. That was smart. Ads featured people desperate for a glass of milk, usually after hastily downing a bunch of chocolate chip cookies or a piece of chocolate cake, only to find when they opened the fridge that they had run out of milk. The campaign launched with a $25 million budget—just for California.[29]

The paid advertising campaign was a hit. It generated so much interest that news outlets began adding value to it by reporting on the campaign itself, at no cost to the CMPB. Over the ensuing six years, the paid media campaign generated more nonpaid media coverage than any other ad campaign in history.[30]

More important, the campaign exceeded its goals. In May 1994, just seven months after the campaign began, the *Los Angeles Times* reported that it had "developed a near cult following" and quoted Manning: "For the first time in years, milk consumption in the state is up among teen-agers and young adults."[31] In an unintended benefit of the campaign, the number of California households stating that they used milk increased from 70 percent of households in 1993 to 74 percent in 1995.[32] A tracking study showed that between October 1994, before the campaign began, and the end of 1995, "the average number of occasions on which people claimed to use milk had risen from 3.9 times in the past 24 hours, to 4.3 times."[33] In all but the first two months of the campaign, milk consumption had increased over the previous year. In 1998, John Steel recapped the campaign results in his book *Truth, Lies, and Advertising*: "Where California had previously trailed the rest of the United States in per capita and household milk consumption, it quickly overhauled the other states and has since extended its lead. As consumption in the rest of the United States continued to decline, it provided further confirmation that something different was going on in California."[34]

While the immediate goal for the campaign had been to stem the decline in milk sales, Steel reported that it actually began to increase milk sales over the prior year by 5.2 million gallons, or 0.7 percent. It was, he continued, "the first increase in milk sales recorded anywhere in the United States in the last decade."[35]

An advertising investment that could produce a 0.7 percent increase in charitable giving in the United States would generate $2.1 billion in new donation revenue.

In the "Got Milk?" campaign's fourth year, sales continued to appear to be on the rise.[36]

The difference between what the industry would have lost between 1993 and 1998 had it not run the campaign and what it gained by running the campaign was estimated at about 75 million gallons, or $187.5 million (at 1998 prices of $2.50 per gallon). That's quite a return for a $25 million investment.

As a result of the campaign's success, Dairy Management, the national equivalent of the CMPB, picked up the ball from California, licensed the campaign, and launched it nationwide with an $80 million annual media budget. The national campaign garnered positive results consistent with the first year of the campaign in California.[37]

By 1996, awareness for the campaign was at an unbelievable 91 percent.[38] Marketing Case Studies reported, "A 1999 national survey revealed that awareness for the tagline 'Got Milk?' was 12 times greater than the slogan for Pepsi, 6 times greater than the sports drink Gatorade's tagline 'Life's a sport. Drink it up,' and 4 times greater than Coke's slogan 'Enjoy.' . . . In 2003 the CMPB reported that the campaign had a 97 percent awareness rate in California."[39]

The "Got Milk?" Facebook page has 40,721 likes.[40]

If an $80 million per year nationwide campaign produced those kinds of results, then something on that order, about $110 million in 2010 adjusted dollars, is probably the minimum level of annual spending we should be considering.

"It's Too Expensive!"

I can already see some people jumping up and down in a rage over the notion that we would spend $110 million a year to advertise the humanitarian sector. I can hear them saying that donors will be outraged. I disagree. Some people will be outraged. But I generally find that the people prone to outrage when it comes to contributing to causes are looking for a good excuse not to give. Let's not waste our time trying to please them.

And let's reframe what is big and what is not. America donates $300 billion annually to charity: $110 million is .036 percent of $300 billion—three one-hundredths of 1 percent. The idea of not spending three one-hundredths of 1 percent of the $300 billion donated to charity each year—three pennies out of every one hundred dollars—to educate the public about how that money can be used to maximum benefit and to attempt to dramatically increase their giving: that is what should have people jumping up and down in a rage.

The humanitarian sector's reference points are all off. It has been so intimidated and oppressed by hundreds of years of insistence on deprivation that it has no understanding of what big actually is. It lives in this miniature world, with, as Susan Berresford of the Ford Foundation calls them, "miniaturized ambitions."

Imagine

Imagine that you wake up one morning, open your paper or digital *New York Times*, *San Francisco Chronicle*, or *Chicago Tribune*, and see a full-page ad, right up front, in the main news section (Figure 3.2). It features a very tight, close-up shot of someone

Figure 3.2 "I'm Overhead" Advertisement, Breast Cancer Alliance

who works for a local, well-known humanitarian organization, his eyes looking straight into yours. Next to him there's a giant headline: **"I'm overhead."** The body copy reads:

> I manage fundraising for the Breast Cancer Alliance. My job is to get more people to give so that our researchers can do more to find a cure. My salary gets labeled as "overhead," as if the work I do doesn't go to the cause. But without the work I do and the money I raise, there is no cause. My sister died of breast cancer. That's why I do this work. I'm committed to the cause every bit as much as the doctors who do the research. I work on "the cause" every hour of the day, every day of the week. Overhead gets a bad rap. My name is Martin Hodges. I'm committed to ending breast cancer, and I'm overhead.

At the bottom of the ad is this line:

> Charity Defense Council. Changing the way we think about changing the world.

It's not a quarter-page or a half-page ad. It's full page. And it's not donated. It's paid for, so that it goes right up front next to the ad for BMW and the latest Sprint special. No one can miss it. It isn't buried in hand-me-down remnant space at the back of the sports section, where so many charity communications go to die.

Now imagine that you wake up the next day and see another full-page ad just like it, featuring a different person—perhaps an executive director or a director of impact and evaluation making the same case. Then you turn on the radio as you drive into the office and this ad comes on:

> I'm overhead. I manage the office for Hunger No More. My job is to run the operation smoothly, so that our team can

> focus on new strategies for ending chronic malnutrition in kids. My salary gets labeled as "overhead," as if the work I do is not part of the cause, or steals from the cause. But if the office doesn't run smoothly, that undermines the cause. I care about hungry kids. That's why I do this work. And I have a wife and three children who depend on me to earn a good living. I'm as committed to the cause every bit as much as the doctors who do the research. I work on the cause every hour of the day, every day of the week. Overhead gets a bad rap. My name is Anthony Rodriguez. I'm committed to ending hunger, and I'm overhead.

And imagine that you walk down the stairs to the subway one day and see five large placards, each featuring a large photo of a different person, each with the headline, "I'm overhead," and each telling the story of his or her subject. You get on the subway and see more placards with the same message. You walk out of the subway station and see a billboard with that message. You log onto CNN or Facebook and you see banner ads with that message. You see a person walking down the street with a T-shirt that says, "I'm overhead." You see bumper stickers on cars saying the same.

You see this all year long.

The next year we tackle public distaste for expenditures on fundraising. You open up your favorite magazine on your iPad and see an ad that looks similar to the "I'm overhead" ads. It features an older woman looking directly into camera. But this time the message says, "I don't want to be the only donor." The body copy reads:

> Eight years ago my grandson died of leukemia. Ever since then, I've been donating to Cure Leukemia. The only way Cure Leukemia is ever going to grow is with more donors. To

> get more donors, it has to spend money doing it. Budweiser spends money to get more people to drink beer. If Cure Leukemia, and other charities like it, can't spend money on fundraising and advertising, they can't get more donors. They can't grow. And they can't do things like cure leukemia. My name is Barbara Stanton. I want the charities I support to spend money getting other donors. Because I don't want to be the only donor.

And just like the "I'm overhead" campaign, you start to see the "I don't want to be the only donor" ads and messages all over your world.

There are other creative ways to get the public thinking in new ways about these issues. We have to go after the sacred cows—indeed, make those sacred cows speak on our behalf.

What tugs at people's hearts more than a child doing something good for charity? Traditionalists could build their entire emotional case on the back of an eight-year-old kid with a piggy bank full of pennies she's going to donate to charity. So imagine an ad featuring that same little girl walking toward the camera with her piggy bank. She is comically sophisticated. She says:

> I have been saving all of my birthday money for two years to give to charity. I am giving it to the Hope Soup Kitchen. But I don't want them to spend it on soup. I want them to spend it on fundraising professionals. Because I want Hope to grow. I want Hope to be able to serve soup to everyone who needs it, not just the few they can afford to serve it to. And the only way they can do that is to invest more money in raising money. So here are my pennies and my dimes. Please invest them—all of them—in fundraising.

No adult wants to think she has a less sophisticated view of charity than a six-year-old child, right? This campaign could be repeated with a senior citizen on a fixed income or a person living below the poverty line who contributes to a favorite charity whatever he can on a regular basis—in other words, the most sympathetic characters imaginable, expressing the most straightforward common sense to the general public.

We can run campaigns in which we promote the specific results of charities. Others can educate people about giving more intelligently, offering helpful questions to ask when considering a new charity. Or imagine a year of ads featuring respected celebrities telling the public they want their donations to go to leadership and fundraising so that their favorite charities can grow.

The possibilities are unending and exciting. Can you imagine walking into a world with this kind of advertising? It's a whole new world. It's the start of a conversation we've never had with the public.

What About Social Media? Are They All They're Cracked Up to Be?

Yes and no. If you're trying to get a date, yes. If you're trying to change the way the general public thinks about charity, and compete with the likes of Exxon Mobil, and planning not to spend any money, not so much.

The figures that we looked at above comparing charity advertising with consumer brand advertising included paid online media. So the disparities hold true online as well as offline. Zero is zero, no matter how many different ways you add it up, no matter how many different outlets on which you spend it. The zero the sector spends on any collective message is zero whether you're talking about online media or not.

Social media are still being defined, and there aren't hard-and-fast rules, but in my mind, they break down into these categories:

- Games
- The blogosphere, and the interaction that goes on among people when they comment on millions of blogs every day
- Online news, and the interaction that goes on among people when they comment on millions of news stories every day
- Facebook, Twitter, YouTube, and other social networking sites, including chat rooms, bulletin boards, and listservs that charities may operate on their sites
- Web applications and sites that promote some kind of action or activity that isn't necessarily conversational in nature—for example, Instagram, Flickr, or Groupon or, in the case of our sector, DonorsChoose, or Crowdrise, or Gulf Coast Gives (which my company created); people also communicate through their actions
- Online stores like iTunes or Amazon that allow you to share your favorite music with your friends or comment on or rate purchases
- Consumer feedback sites like Yelp
- Promotional and educational Web sites, including charity Web sites

Nonpaid social media, regardless of category, are not substitutes for paid media, online or offline. Of course, if you have the one-in-a-million social media idea that hits, social media may do the trick entirely, for a while. But if you're not and if you're hoping and praying that social media can relieve you of the need to spend money to attract customers, you're going to be left without any. They'll be getting scooped away from you from those who recognize the value of media spending.

But here's the big thing: paradoxically, "nonpaid" social media aren't free. If you're serious about engaging in social media, you have to put resources into it. If you want a successful Facebook page, you have to drive people to it (probably through paid advertising of some sort) and keep pushing content to it. Someone has to create or fund that content. Someone has to track the analytics on it to see what content is drawing people and what isn't. Someone has to mine the results of this effort.

A 2009 report from Forrester Research states, "More than 50% of interactive marketers say they will increase their spending on social marketing. Why? These inexpensive tools can quickly get marketing messages out through interactive discussion and rapid word of mouth and, properly managed, can deliver measurable results."[41] According to a 2011 survey of one hundred business-to-business companies commissioned by Worldcom Public Relations Group, the world's leading partnership of independently owned PR firms, 54 percent plan to increase spending on social media in 2011.[42] In both of these findings, the operative phrase is "increase spending." If you want social media to be effective, you can't spend nothing on it.

The August 2011 Chief Marketing Officer Survey, which queried about 250 companies with annual revenues ranging from $25 million to more than $100 billion, found that at the median, chief marketing officers planned to take social media spending from 7.1 percent of the marketing budget to 17.5 percent of the budget over the next five years. That tells us that they find social media productive but, again, only if they spend serious money on these media.[43]

Roland Csaki, of World Wildlife Federation, summed up the real point in speaking at the International Fundraising Conference in 2011: "Just having a big Facebook fan base means nothing. You have to build a strategy to drive them to your site."[44] And that costs money.

These days, you can't go to a conference in the humanitarian sector at which "free" social media isn't promoted as the second coming and you aren't asked to suffer through half a day listening to someone with a PowerPoint on it. No time is devoted to paid media. There are no tracks on the value of online display ads, television, and radio ads.

Here's the problem with the sector's hype about social media: people will do almost anything to keep the status quo in place. That includes keeping in place the big fat zero the sector spends on advertising. So the bright idea gets promoted that, *Hey, maybe we don't have to spend any money on ads. Let's use social media! It's free!*

And the result?

An August 2011 story in the *Chronicle of Philanthropy*, "Most Charities Still Do Not Raise Much Money via Social Media," reported that only 79 of about 150 large charities said they were raising funds with social media, and just one reported raising a substantial amount.[45] Even that can be deceiving. Facebook may be used, for example, to drive donations to participants in a walkathon. But without the walkathon, there wouldn't be any driver, so the charity still has to go to the expense of financing the walk in order to get Facebook to produce.

Those that do have success with social media do so because they spend money on it. That same *Chronicle* story noted that the National Multiple Sclerosis Society of New York spent "about

$50,000 to hire social-media experts to train a corps of staff members who were then encouraged to teach the rest of the organization's employees how to incorporate social media into their work."[46] So there's the $50,000 expense, and then there's the opportunity cost of the worker's paid time going into driving traffic to social media instead of other activities. Again, even "free" social media are not free, and the amount of money that an organization should put into these media has to be measured against their productivity and the productivity of the other forms of paid media available to it.

Remember that Disney has social media available to it as well. So do Budweiser, L'Oréal, Mars Candy, milk, eggs, pork, and every other consumer brand and industry on the planet. Remember how many Facebook likes the oil industry had? That doesn't stop their members from collectively spending hundreds of billions of dollars a year on paid advertising.

A Web site (for the Charity Defense Council, for example) won't drive traffic to itself. You have to let people know about it. And, yes, you can let people know through Facebook. But that's not going to do much if you have only seventy-nine friends. Should you do it? Yes, of course. Why let seventy-nine contacts go to waste? But a Superbowl ad will put you in touch with half a billion contacts. So we should be doing that too. And we should be measuring the cost per lead of the Superbowl ad against the cost per lead for an investment in social media. Either way, you're talking about an investment. It's not free.

Social media are complements to paid advertising. We should exploit social media to the full measure of their potential. But that doesn't obviate the need for us to get serious about competing with the rest of the economy with paid online and offline advertising.

In Summary: What We Need to Build

We must begin to speak in the media and spend whatever resources are necessary to get our message across. It is our civic duty to correct the pervasive public misperception of the humanitarian sector because we're the only ones who know the truth. If we rise to this challenge, we can achieve three goals at once: come out of our own shells, do the public a great service, and advance our causes and all of the human beings affected by them.

Achieving these goals will be one of the chief functions of the Charity Defense Council. To succeed, the organization must develop proficiencies in research, message creation, and execution.

Research and Understand Our Public

We have to begin by understanding what the public thinks about the sector and why. We cannot simply assume. The messages we develop and the media purchases we make cannot be based on faulty assumptions. Older generations may think differently about these issues than younger generations do. There may be regional differences and differences across religious and political persuasions. People may hold an opinion about the charity they love that is wildly different from their opinion about charities in general. We need to know these things in order to be effective. And with the exception of a few now-dated surveys that measured public perception of the sector in the past, we don't have a great deal of information.

But we must be careful about going overboard here. And our sector loves to go overboard when it comes to gathering data in advance of any action. In fact, it often substitutes the gathering of data for the taking of action. If Disneyland were ever constructed as a "nonprofit" enterprise, we'd still be gathering the data on it. We'd still be studying whether we think people from the East Coast will buy a plane ticket to Anaheim and spend $129 for an admission ticket. It would be decades away from ever being built. The humanitarian sector has it all backward. We obsess over gathering data before we act. The for-profit sector, by contrast, acts in order to gather data. You can't gather data in a vacuum. You have to start doing things and measuring the data those things produce. Otherwise you don't have any data. And you never will.

We generally know that the public has a lower-than-low opinion of us. We now need to find out a little more about that public sentiment and understand its nuances across various demographics and psychographics. But this cannot be a pretext for questioning whether to proceed with the whole enterprise. Our approval ratings are lower than those of Congress. We need to act, and now.

We also need to conduct research to establish baselines against which we can measure things in the future to see if we're actually changing public opinion.

Here's some of what we need to know:

- What percentage of Americans currently think the sector wastes money? How does the public define waste?
- How do Americans rate the sector in terms of its effectiveness? Its integrity?
- How do those figures break down by geography, demographics, and psychographics?
- Why do people think what they think? What has influenced them?
- What do they think "overhead" means?
- What do they think "impact" means? "Effectiveness"? How do they define these words?

- Does the public draw distinctions between fundraising costs and administrative costs?
- What compensation levels do they think are too high for a charity leader, and why?
- When asked whether they'd be willing to see more spent on overhead if it meant the problem would get solved more quickly, how do they respond?
- When asked whether they would tolerate much higher levels of leadership compensation if it meant the social issue in question could get addressed much more quickly, how do they respond?
- When asked if they would tolerate much higher levels of fundraising spending in the short term if it meant their favorite organizations could grow much larger, how do they respond?
- How do people feel about the sector starting to defend itself?

Armed with answers to these questions, we can bring much more powerful creativity to bear on the messages we design. Creativity is at its best when it really understands the problem.

We'll need strong ongoing research capability in order to conduct quantitative research (surveys, for example), qualitative research (interviews and focus groups), and public opinion polling. This research will allow us to measure the progress we're making and must be a permanent feature of our work.

Get the Message Right

We have to develop great campaigns in response to what we learn from the data. They should be fun, stimulating, thoughtful, impassioned, and provocative. The public should look forward to reading and seeing the materials developed. They should win awards. They should invigorate our sector too. With about 10 million people working in the sector in the United States, that workforce is actually a substantial subset of our overall audience.

Obviously every part of the advertising equation is critical: the media plan, the amount to be spent on it, and the message. A breakdown in any one of these areas kills the whole effort. But ultimately the power of the creative is what will make the ads effective. Money thrown at bad creative, i.e., bad messaging, is not money worth spending. California milk processors learned that the hard way with campaigns they ran prior to the "Got Milk?" campaign. Those previous campaigns were dull, focusing on the health benefits of milk (I'll bet you don't remember, "Milk, it does a body good"), and the public could have cared less.

The smartest thing that the California Milk Processing Board did was to conduct an exhaustive search for the firm that could meet its challenge. And it didn't hire the largest one. In fact, the agency that came up with "Got Milk?" was small. But they got the client and they understood the challenge. There was a meeting not of minds but of spirits. In the same way, when Steve Jobs returned to Apple in 1997, he knew that Apple's public image needed, if not a makeover, a reassertion. Its original image as a rebellious, iconoclastic champion of possibility had gotten lost in a decade of cautious, unsexy products. A bunch of agencies had been asked to take on the challenge. Jobs hated all of the stuff they put forward. So he called Lee Clow at TBWA/Chiat/Day, who had done the famous "1984" ad for the Mac, in which a lone heroine smashes the huge screen on which Big Brother is speaking to the indoctrinated masses. Clow and his team came up with the iconic "Think Different" campaign that featured rebels as diverse as Gandhi, Einstein, Martin Luther King Jr., and even Lucille Ball and Ricky Ricardo. This campaign reintroduced the

Apple brand and set it on the path to become the world's most valuable company.

The agency is our voice. It must be as rebellious and impassioned as we are.

The campaign on TV or radio or in print is just the beginning. It's the call to action. We also need to think about the action. If we run the "I'm overhead" campaign discussed above and find that people respond well to it—that they want to get further engaged—we'll need a set of tools that will help them to do that. Those tools will have to include:

- *A Web site.* It has to build on the momentum that the ads generate.
- *Other online tools.* We have to arm people with the tools they need to spread the word. They have to be fun to use and so powerful that users will be proud and excited to send them around to their friends.
- *Grassroots organizing tools.* Do people need a slide show that they can download to do a presentation to their own friends? Do they want posters? T-shirts? Banners for organizing an event at their organization? All of these collateral materials need to be built on the campaign that got people interested in the first place. They all have to be of a piece.
- *Public-interfacing administrative tools.* What's the on-hold programming saying when people call into the office after watching one of our ads? What's the sign on the front of the building? Is there a campaign message on our letterhead? We cannot be arguing for equality with the for-profit sector in marketing and then model something less than that. Banana Republic would never allow a store employee to scratch out a "Back in five minutes" sign on the front door of the store. Neither will we.

Execute Effectively

Execution of marketing is where I see most humanitarian organizations fall down. They spend months getting board approval for a modest marketing effort (which usually doesn't include any money to buy media), more months deciding on the right vendor, and more months deciding on the right message, and then they think the work is done. In fact, the work has only just begun. Far too few organizations look at the marketing effort the way that they should: like a political campaign. In a political campaign, developing the message is step 1 in a continuum of one hundred steps. Once you have the message and even after you start running ads, the real work of translating all of that into votes begins. This requires a war room, with real human beings, where progress is tracked on giant data boards that everyone can see. How many new volunteers did we get today? How many leaflets did they drop? How many house parties have we conducted? How much did they raise?

In other words, you have to create a machine to execute the media campaign, channel all of the responses to it into a multitude of real actions, measure those actions, and adjust your behavior on the basis of what the measurements are telling you. This critical part of the overall effort is usually completely overlooked. In our effort, we will treat it with the respect that it deserves.

We will need a test city for an initial campaign. Should it be a small city, where media costs are lower, where it's less expensive to make a splash, and easier to control things? Should it be Washington, D.C., so that we can educate national policymakers—the president even—immediately? Should we start in a city with a subway system, in which our audience will be more captive? Is there a funder somewhere that might foot the bill for the first campaign if we run it in that funder's home town? These questions must be answered.

There's an enormous opportunity to integrate what we're doing with a number of other component parts that will make the entire effort much more productive than the media would be simply on their own. Two of the biggest additional components will be nonpaid media efforts and the engagement of local humanitarian organizations and their staffs, boards, donors, and supporters. Accordingly, we must engage a world-class public relations agency so that nonpaid media can supplement the power of the paid media. If we can get front-page stories in major metropolitan papers for free covering the ambitious goals we have for changing the way the public thinks about us and our provocative campaign, it will dramatically leverage the power of the paid media and give us exactly the kind of story we want, that is, the humanitarian sector finally standing up for itself.

Also, we'll fully engage local humanitarian agencies to conduct educational campaigns with their constituencies during the campaign period and provide them with the tools to do so. Running a great ad campaign is one thing. But the impact is much greater if the people who see the campaign on television then also see it on posters when they go to donate clothing to Goodwill, or on the front of a solicitation envelope that comes to them from some other charity they support. And if the campaign has a great presence at local charities, it reinforces the message for the people who work there.

We'll develop community programs to educate the public in more high-touch ways: offer lunch break seminars to local businesses or test-drive a curriculum for high school seniors, college students, and even the staff of our humanitarian organizations.

These efforts can take people much deeper into the issues than we'll be able to go with advertising alone.

Finally, we have to measure the impact of all of this. That means building a solid research and evaluation department, which will gather and analyze data, then make recommendations to the rest of the organization based on what it's learning. This research will include ongoing and postcampaign public opinion polling to measure changes, and ongoing and postcampaign polling of local humanitarian organizations to measure the impact at their level, especially on giving. Ultimately increasing giving is a big part of what this is all about.

In Conclusion

If we dedicate ourselves to this effort, we can have a general public with a far more sophisticated view of what it takes to solve social problems—a public that thinks highly of the sector and understands the work that it does, the challenges it faces, and the resources it requires to solve problems. We can reorient people to addressing problems rather than reviewing overhead ratios and financials and get them genuinely excited about the prospect of actually solving those problems. We can build a society that does much more giving because it is educated about and genuinely engaged in all of these things.

Instead of saying, "The money never gets to the people who need it," it will say, "I think the humanitarian sector is the best feature of our society."

4

Build a Legal Defense Fund for Charity

The obstacle is the path.
ZEN PROVERB

In February 2011 Oregon's attorney general, John Kroger, introduced Senate Bill 40, which sought to strip the tax-deductible status from donations made to charities that spend less than 30 percent of their annual budget on services over the course of a three-year period. A report in the *Oregonian* stated that the bill "would require affected charities to tell donors that contributions aren't tax-deductible." According to a representative of Kroger's office, "Violators would be subject to a lawsuit for violations of the Unlawful Trade Practices Act," and "they could be sued up to $25,000 per violation. That means any transaction in which they fail to make the right disclosure." Kroger said that the bill is "designed to address a very real and present problem in Oregon. . . . And that is charities that are registered in the state and raising money in the state but go on to do almost no charitable work with the money they raise. Some of these charities are little more than scams."[1]

This sounds like great public policy, doesn't it? What could be wrong with asking charities to spend at least 30 percent of their budgets on their intended purpose? And don't we want to weed out scams? Isn't that what attorneys general should be doing?

Yes. But that's not what this bill would have done.

Unintended Consequences

In 1936 the renowned American sociologist Robert K. Merton wrote a paper while at Harvard entitled, "The Unanticipated Consequences of Purposive Social Action." Its ideas predated him, but the name he gave them—or a modification of it—stuck. Unfortunately, the "law of unintended consequences" aptly applies to much of the public policy, especially at the state and local levels, aimed at humanitarian organizations. Merton recognized that it was not "the inscrutable will of God or Providence or Fate" that led to unanticipated consequences or undesirable outcomes, but rather, human intervention in complicated systems we don't fully understand—and in some cases, we don't know that we don't fully understand.[2]

In other words, the best intentions can produce the most perverse effects, possibly fundamentally at odds with their initial intent. For example, giving free mosquito nets to poor people in developing countries might sound like a good thing, until you realize that in addition to thwarting mosquitoes, you're killing the jobs of poor people who were previously making a meager living selling mosquito nets to their neighbors. Buying cheap T-shirts for the local hunger walk might sound like a great way of reducing costs, until you realize that the shirts were produced by the rural poor in sweatshops in Bangladesh, adding misery to the poverty they already experience and creating the need for a whole new walk-a-thon just to combat the effects of the first one.

In the papers he was writing at the time, Merton listed five possible causes of unanticipated consequences:

- *Ignorance.* The "exigencies of practical life frequently compel us to act with some confidence even though it is manifest that the information on which we base our action is not complete. We usually act . . . not on the basis of scientific knowledge, but opinion and estimate."[3]
- *Error.* "In our appraisal of the present situation . . . in our selection of a course of action, or . . . the execution of the action chosen [or believing] . . . that actions which have in the past led to the desired outcome will continue to do so."[4]
- *Immediate interest.* As opposed to long-term interest, or "instances where the actor's paramount concern with the foreseen immediate consequences excludes the consideration of further other consequences of the same act."[5]
- *Basic values.* Instances where there is no consideration of further consequences because of the felt necessity of certain action enjoined by certain fundamental values."[6]
- *Self-defeating prophecy.* "The counterpart of the self-fulfilling prophecy is the self-defeating or 'suicidal' prophecy which so alters human behavior from what would have been its course had it not been made, that it fails to be borne out."[7]

I might add *political expediency* to the list.

All of these problems apply to humanitarian sector public policy. They not only produce unintended effects but fail to produce intended outcomes. I could say they don't produce the outcomes they were designed to produce, except that they are usually written without any design. They are more the result of emotion and ignorance than of thoughtful design.

There is no shortage of examples of these. And there is no shortage of examples of newly elected (and, in some cases, veteran) city council members, state representatives, city managers, city attorneys, and state attorneys general who know little or nothing about the realities of humanitarian sector business practice. Yet they are all fired up to put new regulations into place in the name of protecting the public interest.

As with anti-defamation and paid advertising, the humanitarian sector lacks an overarching, visionary, and well-funded strategy to deal with this issue. It also lacks an entity specifically committed to taking this issue on at the level required. But the massive opportunities that exist in long-term, national, strategic plans for anti-defamation and advertising intersect with the opportunity that exists for a long-term, national, strategic response to bad public policy. Together these three initiatives could combine to create a defense and promotion of the sector unlike anything we've ever imagined.

But let's start by looking at the present and at specific examples of seemingly good public policy that have produced bad side effects. Let's begin by looking at what's wrong with the proposed Oregon law, which seems so smart on its face.

First, the proposal uses a false theory of transparency. It assumes that disclosure of overhead equates to transparency. Nothing could be further from the truth. Many reported overhead ratios distort and obscure the truth. They obscure the underlying accounting that goes into calculating the overhead percentage. How? The percentage of donations that a charity uses for "the cause" depends entirely on how its accounting defines "the cause." The more broadly it defines it, the higher the percentage it can tell everyone is going to it, regardless of whether the charity's definition is much broader than the general public's.

For example, the charity might say that its cleaning service is part of the cause. By doing that, it can tell the public that a higher percentage of donations goes to the cause. But the public might not agree that cleaning the office is part of the cause.

Reporting a high rate of overhead may actually signal a kind of innocence: that the charity isn't using accounting shenanigans to lower the figure. So the proposed Oregon legislation drives right past the real potential for fraud in the form of fraudulent accounting. Charities that use aggressive, even unethical, accounting practices to mask high overhead get a free pass—or worse, they're made to look good. This practice is widespread. The Nonprofit Overhead Cost Project at Indiana University reported that of 126,956 tax forms they studied, half of the organizations reported a hard-to-believe 0 percent fundraising cost, and one-quarter of charities with revenues between $1 million and $5 million reported a 0 percent fundraising cost.[8]

Also, there is no standard definition for a fundraising cost ratio. Some define it as the percentage of money spent on fundraising divided by money spent on programs. That calculation overlooks money raised but not spent—for example, to create cash reserves, fund an endowment, or fund a capital campaign.[9]

So the proposed law is actually not delivering true transparency to law enforcement. The fact that law enforcement believes that it is will result in it overlooking organizations that aren't being truly transparent and may accuse those that are. But another unintended consequence is that it sends the wrong definition of "transparency" to the public. It reinforces bad analysis and bad judgment.

The big issue here isn't about transparency. It's about makers of public policy creating regulations for the sector without understanding the effects of what they're proposing.

Second, it inaccurately equates high overhead with fraud. Whether a charity spends more or less than 30 percent of donations on services is no indication of misconduct. The proposed law was dysfunctional: it had a blind spot for real fraud and put a spotlight on potential innocence. The U.S. Supreme Court recognized this fallacy. In May 2003 the Court issued this opinion in support of a previous finding by the Illinois Supreme Court: "The Illinois Supreme Court in the instant case correctly observed that 'the percentage of [fundraising] proceeds turned over to a charity is not an accurate measure of the amount of funds used "for" a charitable purpose.' "[10]

An organization's overhead might be consistently high for many reasons: obscurity of the cause, a long-term strategy at work, educational efforts not labeled as services, and so on. The U.S. Supreme Court said this when it restated its 1984 decision in *Secretary of State of Maryland* v. *Joseph H. Munson Co., Inc.* In that case, a professional fundraiser challenged a statute that prohibited a charity from paying expenses of more than 25 percent for fundraising activity. The court ruled in the fundraiser's favor, saying that if a percentage-based test "actually prevented fraud in some cases it would be 'little more than fortuitous.' "[11] In *Munson*, the Court stated that the statute "operates on a fundamentally mistaken premise that high solicitation costs are an accurate measure of fraud."[12] The *Munson* decision demonstrated "that there is no nexus between the percentage of funds retained by the fundraiser and the likelihood that the solicitation is fraudulent."[13]

Indeed a previous law in Oregon that prohibited charities from soliciting if they spent too much on administration and fundraising was rendered unconstitutional after a Supreme Court ruling that such provisions threaten freedom of speech. It was repealed by the Oregon legislature in 1989.[14]

So the problem is bigger than state officials not understanding the dynamics of fraud in charity. They are unaware of previous Supreme Court rulings on the subject and even of public policy history in their own state. This is why the sector needs a powerful, well-funded entity focused on public policy.

Third, it undermines the potential for growth. Humanitarian organizations must begin achieving exponential growth. To do that, they must invest substantially in fundraising. Since these investments usually take more than three years to bear fruit, the proposed law creates a huge disincentive to pursue the kind of growth needed to solve entrenched social problems. The legislation makes an exception for capital campaigns, so it recognizes that to build a building, you have to spend years raising money before work on design and construction can begin. The same principle should apply to building major social movements and progress.

The issue here is not the academics of revenue development. It's the fact that policymakers don't understand the academics of revenue development, and yet they make public policy as if they do.

Fourth, it discriminates against the most disadvantaged causes. The legislation would punish charities that have obscure causes that are much harder to raise funds for than popular causes. A cause like achondroplasia (dwarfism), which affects one in 25,000 people worldwide, is enormously more difficult and expensive to raise money for than a cause like breast cancer, for which one in every two people is potentially at risk.[15]

Related to this, the law reinforces bad analysis of telemarketing, which is sometimes the only fundraising option available to less popular causes. Often we hear that a telemarketing firm takes 90 percent of what it raises. We are aghast: "They're getting rich while no money is going to the cause!" If that were true, there'd be a lot more people in the telemarketing business. But it's an amateur analysis that ignores the telemarketer's costs. A firm might make 100 calls and get 100 "no, thank yous." On the 101st call, someone donates ten dollars. So the firm makes nine dollars for 101 calls. Not very profitable. The fact that it charges 90 percent of donations doesn't mean it's making a 90 percent profit. Indeed, it could be losing money. The percentage it takes out of a donation is not a gauge of its profitability.

Often it is the lesser-known causes that have to resort to this form of fundraising. In many cases the telemarketing firm will essentially advance the upfront costs: it will take the financial risk associated with the possibility of zero donations and accept payment on the basis of only those people who do contribute, eliminating the need for the charity to invest in staff, space, telephony, and technology. That's attractive to a cause for which it is traditionally very difficult to raise funds. It's also extremely attractive to an organization that has no capital with which to launch its fundraising efforts.

Fifth, it discourages the most creative thinkers. The legislation would favor big, older institutions that have established fundraising engines and would punish new entrepreneurial efforts that don't, despite the fact that the newer efforts might have better problem-solving ideas.

Sixth, it creates a dangerous precedent. Once a law is in place that requires a certain level of spending on programs, what's to prevent amending it to require a higher level? Better Business Bureau's Wise Giving Alliance standards call for organizations to spend no more than 35 percent of their expenses on fundraising.[16] What's to prevent the state of Oregon from aligning with the Better Business Bureau? On its face, we can see how the idea might be immediately embraced by the general public.

Finally, by focusing exclusively on overhead ratios, the law enshrines the ratios as a panacea, putting Oregon legislation at odds with leading thought on the matter. While every thoughtful voice is urging the public to stop asking about overhead, Oregon would be counseling its citizens to do the opposite.

But Oregon's attorney general was apparently unaware of this. He would not have been had the sector had an entity and strategy in place that was proactive and that was educating and building relationships with his office.

As a result of fragmented and frantic pressure placed on the state by local advocates and national writers, including me, the state has abandoned the proposed legislation, at least for now.[17] The *Oregonian* reported that state representative Vicki Berger "said it would create bad publicity for nonprofits and cast suspicion on charities that have good reasons for high expenses," and that "others say the bill's reliance solely on financial documents is unfair."[18] This is a happy example of education making a difference.

But the legislation never should have been proposed in the first place. Its proposal had the negative effect of stirring up and broadcasting negative public sentiment about our sector.

More Bad Policy Cloaked in Good Rhetoric

Oregon is not alone, and overhead ratios are not the only target of public policy.

Newcomers to elected office and old-timers alike regularly react to news reports about charitable organizations and, in response, propose ill-conceived new investigations, regulations, and laws. We have seen the unintended consequences of Senator

Chuck Grassley and Governor Andrew Cuomo's actions on Boys & Girls Clubs donors and New York charitable organizations.

It has gotten worse. Andrew Cuomo's witch hunt evolved into misguided public policy. On January 3, 2012, the New York State Senate Standing Committee on Investigations and Government Operations posted notice of a public hearing: "To examine executive compensation at not-for-profit organizations receiving State funding and the actions needed to prevent State tax dollars from being wasted on excessive salaries." The committee sent a press release that stated: "In 2010, the Division of the Budget found that at not-for-profit organizations under contract with State mental hygiene agencies there were 1,926 employees with salaries greater than $100,000. . . . It is unconscionable that funds that could be providing badly needed services are spent instead on bloated management salaries."[19]

In fact, the hearing hadn't even been held before these conclusions that salaries are bloated were made. Why even have a hearing? It's the dollar amount itself that is deemed conclusive; the question of whether the people served by these organizations were better off as a result of the investment was not even get raised. And what a double standard. The Empire Center for New York State Policy shows 116,819 people on state, city, county, and public authority payrolls in 2010 in New York who made at least $100,000. These included the head basketball coach at the State University of New York at Binghamton ($1,026,793), a professor at the State University of New York at Albany for ten months ($793,200), at least a dozen "senior stationary engineers" at the Department of Environmental Protection (each earning more than half a million dollars), and the athletics director at the State University of New York at Buffalo ($355,040). I could list hundreds more.[20]

But it's the leaders at charities who are being singled out.

Before the hearings had even been held, Governor Cuomo reached a conclusion: his 2012/2013 budget requires organizations providing services to the state to ensure that "at least 85 percent of every public dollar will be spent on direct services, not administration." That's up from the state's historic requirement of 75 percent, which itself was onerous. In addition, "reimbursement for any executive's compensation will be capped at $199,000. Excess compensation will be a basis for rejection of a provider."[21]

What if 85 percent expenditure on programs and only 15 percent spent on administration leads to inferior programs because of inadequate staff training, inadequate fundraising to support the program, and high turnover at the administrative level because of low salaries, leading to a sense of instability, inconsistency, and high dissatisfaction among program workers? What if the $199,000 cap means a charity has to let a great leader go and trade that person in for an inferior one? Who determines what's excessive?

The notion that we should set salary ranges for state-funded basketball coaches five times higher than what we set for leaders committed to ending homelessness really says everything about public policymakers' illiteracy or obliviousness on what it takes to solve social ills.

If Governor Cuomo wanted to suffocate his humanitarian service providers and ensure the persistence of the state's social problems, he found the perfect way to do it. But that's not what he wanted. He simply didn't know the potential unintended consequences of his actions. In large part, public policymakers don't know what they're doing because the humanitarian sector has cowered before them instead of educated them.

This dynamic has an effect. A 2012 report in the *Chronicle of Philanthropy* citing the results of a *Chronicle* survey stated that an "overwhelming majority of nonprofit employees wish to escape their current jobs."[22] Forty-three percent of respondents were looking for new jobs, and another 39 percent said they would be if the economy were stronger. This is the effect of sucking all of the resources out of an organization. One worker interviewed at a mental health facility in Chicago noted the effects: "We're all generalists now. . . . Our roles just keep expanding." This is what happens when the state is averse to compensating its humanitarian sector workforce without understanding the consequences of its prejudice.

Geoffrey Peters, head of American Charities for Reasonable Fundraising Regulation (ACFRFR) says it better: "It is nearly impossible to [quantify] the number of wrongheaded ideas that make their way into the halls of state and local legislative bodies on a monthly basis."[23] These ideas know no bounds. Between them, they attempt to restrict or regulate every facet of humanitarian sector business practice: funding to build organizational strength, fundraising, efforts to address natural disasters, the ability to hire the right talent, and even an organization's ability to define its mission and impact for the general public.

The humanitarian sector lacks an appropriate response to this public policy reality. We lack a powerful, well-funded, full-time organization dedicated to addressing it strategically over the long term. And what we do have is not integrated with other advertising, anti-defamation, and legislative activities—or with a large national database of advocates that can be brought to bear on each battle. Any effort to overcome bad policy will be most effectively served by such an integrated approach.

It is no surprise, once again, that other communities do have well-funded resources in this area.

The gay and lesbian community has Lambda Legal, with a $15.6 million annual budget. The disabled community has the Disability Rights Education and Defense Fund, with a $1.5 million annual budget.[24] The African American community has the NAACP Legal Defense and Educational Fund, founded by Thurgood Marshall.[25] It has 501(c)(3) status separate from the NAACP itself and a $12.8 million annual budget.[26] The Asian community has the Asian American Legal Defense and Education Fund with a $1.9 million annual budget.[27] The Mexican community has MALDEF, the Mexican-American Legal Defense and Educational Fund, with a $3.6 million annual budget.[28] Each of these organizations protects and fights for the civil and constitutional rights of its communities. We need a well-funded entity to do precisely the same for the humanitarian sector.

Pro Bono Is Not an Ultimate Solution

What we do have is American Charities for Reasonable Fundraising Regulation (ACFRFR). It has no full-time staff and essentially no budget. Its latest Form 990, from 2007, shows annual expenditures of $2,766.[29] It's financed entirely by the goodwill and graces of a few truly heroic attorneys who donate their time as they can on a pro bono basis. Because of funding limitations, it tries to focus on the most egregious cases, but it is unable to respond to every instance. Its last new posting on its Web site was in 2008.

Despite its lack of resources, ACFRFR has been very effective in key cases. Since its formal inception as a public interest law firm in 2006, it has worked on four important cases: two in

Florida, one in Utah, and one in Illinois (the *Madigan* case that was ultimately decided by the U.S. Supreme Court).[30]

Both of the Florida cases involved a proposed ordinance in Pinellas County (in the western part of the state, near Tampa) enacted in 1993.[31] It prescribed three primary regulations: (1) it required fundraising consultants and paid solicitors to register with the county and pay a fee before performing services for the charity, (2) it prohibited a charity from soliciting in the county if it was using a fundraising firm not registered in the county, and (3) it prohibited fundraising firms from soliciting for a charity if the charity itself was not registered with the county.[32] For example, the county tried to get the Diana, Princess of Wales Memorial Fund in the United Kingdom to register in Pinellas County in order to solicit there.[33] Florida already had registration requirements for fundraisers and charities. On January 1, 1992, the Florida Solicitation of Contributions Act took effect regulating solicitation of public contributions and mandating a variety of disclosures.[34] So whether it was intended or not, one of the effects of the proposal would have been to double the amount of administrative work charities and fundraising firms would have to do, an administrative burden that takes money away from program services. There were other unintended potential consequences as well:

- A national firm might decline to help a small Pinellas County charity because of the legal and administrative expense of registering or because of potential civil liabilities. Or it might not want to send national mailings into Pinellas County. The penalty for noncompliance with the ordinance was a civil injunction and possibly a five hundred dollar fine or even imprisonment.[35] One of the ACFRFR members who filed an affidavit in the case (the owner of a fundraising firm) stated that as a direct result of learning of these potential penalties, she advised her clients not to mail into the county and had refused to enter into business agreements with charities that send mail into the county.[36]

- Fundraising firms might decide to charge the charity more because of the administrative hassle of doing business.
- A large national fundraising firm sending out a multimillion-piece mailing, say, for the American Cancer Society, might run afoul of the local ordinance simply because it didn't know about it, which is not a defense in court. It could end up having to defend itself against criminal charges—or, at the very least, deal with the stigmatizing press that might rear its head. The charity itself might get caught up in the legal case, creating a public relations nightmare.
- The ordinance was so broad as to cover copywriters who wrote copy for a national solicitation or graphic designers who did the design for the piece, even though they had no ultimate control over what finally went out, were not involved in the act of the solicitation, and certainly never came close to touching contributions. For example, the plaintiff, Norman Leahy, was a lone copywriter in Richmond, Virginia, who was told he had to register before providing copywriting services to a charity that was going to solicit by mail nationally, including in Pinellas County. A copywriter or graphic designer in, for example, Rhode Island is unlikely to engage in a small assignment that requires registering with Pinellas County, Florida.

But these pale in comparison to the largest potential consequence. Based on the actions of Pinellas County, other municipalities might begin to regard it as their duty to enact similar ordinances. Given the thousands of state, regional, and local jurisdictions in the nation, this would cripple any efforts at centralized, national fundraising solicitation efforts.[37] And in the age of the Internet, it can be argued that anyone with a Web site that can accept donations is participating in a national—really, global—fundraising effort.

The first of the two cases that ACFRFR brought were aimed specifically at the requirements for direct mail firms. ACFRFR argued that the regulation was unnecessary, burdensome, redundant with the state of Florida, and not narrowly tailored to accomplish legitimate municipal government interests: protecting its citizens.[38] More important, ACFRFR argued that the ordinance violated the commerce and due process clauses of the U.S. Constitution for the county by forcing fundraising firms with no offices in, direct business dealings with, or other connections to the county to submit to the county's jurisdiction and allow the county to regulate their out-of-state transactions. In its opinion, the Eleventh Circuit Court of Appeals stated, "A state's legislative jurisdiction is circumscribed by the Due Process Clause: 'There must be at least some minimal contact between a state and the regulated subject before it can, consistently with the requirements of due process, exercise legislative jurisdiction.' "[39] But in this case, the fundraising firms were only assisting charities with mailings within the county, not accepting funds, and not soliciting—the charities were doing the soliciting by mail.[40]

ACFRFR also argued that the ordinance violated the First Amendment rights of charities because it limited charities' ability to speak by limiting the ability of those charities to select professionals in fundraising and communications to help them get their message out as a result of those firms being regulated out-of-state.[41]

ACFRFR won the case on appeal.[42] So rather than having an ordinance on the books that can hobble national fundraising efforts, a precedent has been set that specifically prohibits such ordinances on constitutional grounds.

In a second Pinellas County case, ACFRFR came to the aid of the charities themselves. As a result of the suit, a federal court entered an injunction that prohibited the county from enforcing Internet provisions in the ordinance, an important victory. According to ACFRFR, "Pinellas County subsequently abandoned their entire charity regulation scheme."[43]

On various occasions over the past few years, ACFRFR has sought to extend this important victory in the *Pinellas* case. And it has had success. In one case, the attorney general of California agreed not to enforce a similar section of the state's charitable registration statute. In another, the attorney general of North Dakota agreed not to enforce its statute against out-of-state fundraisers. In a third, the secretary of the state of Oregon agreed to the same stipulation. Local county and city attorneys in Ohio and Kentucky also agreed not to enforce their ordinances and regulations outside their states. ACFRFR also cites numerous instances in which its use of the *Pinellas* case in testimony and correspondence has resulted in legislative counsel in numerous states modifying or defeating legislative proposals to regulate charities.[44]

In a third case, currently pending, ACFRFR has taken action against the state of Utah because of a notorious history of over-regulation and attempts to enforce its statutes outside the boundaries of the state, in the same way that Pinellas County had sought. This case is in the final stages of the discovery process, whereby both sides review documents for the other and depose witnesses.[45]

ACFRFR's most important case was *Madigan* v. *Telemarketing Associates*, which I mentioned earlier. It has been described as "the most significant legal case affecting nonprofits and fundraising in the past decade."[46] In this case, ACFRFR coordinated the filing of three friend-of-the-court briefs, signed by 176 humanitarian organizations. The U.S. Supreme Court unanimously supported the ACFRFR's arguments that there is no nexus between high fundraising cost and the existence of fraud and that the existence of high costs is not misleading in and of itself.[47]

More recently, in summer 2011, the New Jersey Division of Consumer Affairs proposed a regulation that would require charities to advise donors that they can target their gifts to specific programs and provide a mechanism for the designation. In other words, if a donor wanted her ten dollar gift split among fourteen programs, the charity would have to account for seventy-one cents worth of revenue to each program.

The unintended consequences of such a requirement are significant. The accounting expenses associated with that kind of granular allocation for a large quantity of small contributions might well overrun the amount of the contribution itself. Imagine a bookkeeper who is paid twenty dollars an hour having to allocate a ten-dollar gift fourteen different ways. More important, no donor is going to say he wants a portion of his gift to go to overhead, so the proposed regulation would have effectively eliminated overhead funding, regardless of the fact that each program requires overhead to operate. With donations like that, an organization would quickly go bankrupt. The proposed regulation would have applied to "any oral or written solicitation (including a telephonic or electronic solicitation but excluding any in-person solicitation) made by or on behalf of a charitable organization that received contributions of more than $250,000 in its prior fiscal year, which names more than one particular program for which contributions are solicited."[48]

Kansas City attorney Errol Copilevitz, renowned for his landmark defense of the sector's free speech rights (and whose firm graciously prepared the incorporation and tax-exempt filings for the Charity Defense Council on a pro bono basis), drafted a seven-page letter in response to the division's proposal in which he made several arguments against it. First, it would place an undue administrative burden on charities, which would, ironically, increase the charities' administrative costs and thus reduce the amounts it could send to programs. Second, because some donor acquisition efforts net nothing in their infancy, there might not be any net proceeds available to go to programs. Third, the proposal doesn't add to the rights of New Jersey consumers because they already had the right to designate their donations (and charities had an obligation to honor those designations if they accepted the gift). Fourth, the proposal would violate the free speech rights of charities by forcing them to say things they may not wish to say. Copilevitz quoted the U.S. Supreme Court in the decision in *Riley* v. *National Federation of the Blind of North Carolina*: "There is certainly some difference between compelled speech and compelled silence, but in the context of protected speech, the difference is without constitutional significance, for the First Amendment guarantees 'freedom of speech,' a term necessarily comprising the decision of both what to say and what not to say."[49]

Fifty-three charitable organizations and additional trade groups signed on to Copilevitz's letter. ACFRFR also sent the division a letter outlining the arguments against the proposal. As a result, the division, to its credit, withdrew the proposal.

Overall, it sounds as if ACFRFR is doing a great job, and the question might arise, Why do we need anything more? Well, as an initial matter, we have to ask what would have happened if Errol Copilevitz and Geoffrey Peters (who donates most of the litigation and advocacy ACFRFR undertakes in the form of his own time) hadn't been there for the New Jersey case, or if Peters hadn't been there for any of the others. The good intentions of two attorneys do not a national infrastructure make. But more important are all the places that ACFRFR cannot be. For every case in which ACFRFR has been able to come to the rescue, there are a dozen in which it has lacked the time and resources to bring the full force of our rights to bear. Imagine what could be done with a $15 million budget.

Los Angeles, a Case Study

The city of Los Angeles has a particularly egregious disclosure statute that remains on the books and active. If you want to conduct a fundraising effort in Los Angeles, you have to go through the Los Angeles Police Department's Police Commission, Commission Investigation Division, Charitable Services Section. This requirement is in addition to California state registration requirements and the need to have federal tax-exempt status. Fifteen days prior to the beginning of any solicitation, charitable organizations must complete a "Notice of Intention to Solicit Charitable Contributions."

In addition to inquiring about the dates and nature of the solicitation, whether the organization is using a commercial fundraiser, the name of the commercial fundraiser, and whether the fundraiser is being paid a percentage, commission, salary, or other compensation, the form requires that the organization predict and itemize anticipated costs for "Printing, Postage, Stationery (sic), Telephone, Rental—Storeroom, Hall, etc., Rental or

Purchase of Equipment, Reservation Charges ($ _____ per person), Food (Luncheon, Dinner, etc.), Items for Resale Food, Merchandise Decorations, Favors, Prizes, Costumes, Uniforms, Advertising or Publicity Costs, Permits or License Fees, Transportation, Music (Orchestra, etc.), Entertainers, Salaries [and] Additional Expenditures."[50]

What if a charity can't predict what its expenses are going to be because it's a first-time event? And what if the people involved don't want to put their reputations on the line, and incur potential liability, if expenses end up being dramatically different from those they were asked to predict? How can a seven year old raising donations through a lemonade stand know what the cost of her lemonade will be if she has no idea how much of it she will sell?

Imagine if the iPhone came with a police department requirement that Apple predict the associated costs it was going to incur for stationary and food in the development of the device, so that the public could make an informed decision about whether to buy one.

In addition to preparing these estimates, applicants are required to submit "a copy of articles of incorporation, constitution or other rules of operation (including amendments), Copy of bylaws, Copy of Internal Revenue exemption letter, Copy of State Franchise Tax exemption letter, [and] California Charitable Trust Number." The Notice of Intention also says, "The following additional information may be required upon request. (a) Statement of accomplishments for last calendar year. (b) Proposed budget (in detail). (c) Name and location of bank account. Names and titles of persons authorized to sign checks."[51]

Much of this is redundant with what the State of California Attorney General's Registry of Charitable Trusts already requires.

If all is in order, within fifteen days the organization will receive an information card, which it must distribute with each solicitation. According to the Police Department Web site:

> The Los Angeles Municipal Code (LAMC) requires any person or organization soliciting or holding a special event in the City to obtain an Information Card from Charitable Services Section of the Los Angeles Police Commission prior to the event or appeal. The IC provides important information to the donor so they may make an educated decision whether to support that organization. . . . Each solicitor must possess and display upon request a copy of the Information Card to all persons solicited. Mail appeals must contain a replica of the Information Card or the information contained on the card. The Information Card must be displayed at the site of special events.[52]

An organization conducting a solicitation that it has conducted in previous years must report on the information card the results of the previous year's campaign and must show the net return to the charity as a percentage of overall revenue, once again reinforcing the notion of that ratio as a panacea. It provides an example: "2008 activity collected a total of $73,795, of which $7,832 (10.6%) was applied to expenses and $65,963 was donated to charity."[53]

In light of the U.S. Supreme Court's decision in *Riley*, this requirement is unconstitutional on its face because it forces charities to say something they may not wish to say. Perhaps the solicitation is part of a five-year donor recruitment investment, the first year of which may have 100 percent cost. If the charity doesn't have a chance to tell the public, on the information card, what its overall strategic plan is (the whole story), it certainly would not want to tell the public just part of the story (only the first-year costs), leading people to believe that it intends to have 100 percent costs for the duration of the plan.

Moreover, the city of Los Angeles apparently assumes that the public isn't smart enough to do a little investigation of the charities it intends to support. In the *Riley* case, the Supreme Court de facto ruled on this kind of heavy-handed interference by the state when it rejected Illinois's argument that it had a right to interfere on a contract signed between a charity and a fundraiser:

> The State's additional interest in regulating the fairness of the fee may rest on either of two premises (or both): (1) that charitable organizations are economically unable to negotiate fair or reasonable contracts without governmental assistance; or (2) that charities are incapable of deciding for themselves the most effective way to exercise their First Amendment rights. Accordingly, the State claims the power to establish a single transcendent criterion by which it can bind the charities' speaking decisions. We reject both premises.[54]

That's not all. Within thirty days of the completion of the solicitation, charities must file an additional "Report of Results of Activity" detailing all of the revenues and expenses of the event. This is also redundant with what the state of California already requires.[55]

At the bottom of the form are sections on "Total Fundraising Expenses" and "Net Remaining for Charitable Purposes." The "Fundraising Expenses" section requires that the organization itemize all of its expenses for "Salaries, Wages, Commissions (To Whom), Music, Rentals or Purchase of Equipment, Printing, Postage, Stationery (sic), Telephone, Television or Radio Time, Advertising/Publicity Costs, Decorations Favors, Costumes,

Uniforms, Costs of Merchandise, Food, etc., for Resale, Prizes, Reservation Charges, and Other Expenditures (itemize)."[56] The requirement that all of these be categorized as fundraising costs assumes that these expenses have no charitable purpose embedded in them. This assumption is at odds with the U.S. Supreme Court ruling in *Riley*, which stated that "the percentage of [fundraising] proceeds turned over to a charity is not an accurate measure of the amount of funds used 'for' a charitable purpose."[57]

In addition, if the solicitation is by mail, the information card has to be printed and included in the solicitation. This creates a significant additional expense to charities that are preparing large, national, automated mailings. The result is that many charities omit Los Angeles in their mailings, in effect depriving the citizens of Los Angeles of their right to hear what those charities have to say, and the charities are deprived of their right to speak.[58]

If the regulation is unconstitutional, why isn't it challenged?

It has been. In 1992, the Los Angeles County Sheriff's Department raided five properties of Gospel Missions because it believed the organization might be violating city and county charitable solicitation laws.[59] Gospel Missions provides food, shelter, clothes, and financial assistance to the homeless, who join the organization as members and then solicit funds from the general public.[60]

In response to the raid, Gospel Missions sued the city and Los Angeles County, challenging its charitable solicitation laws on constitutional grounds. A district court entered summary judgment in favor of Gospel Missions and enjoined the city and county from enforcing numerous provisions of their respective laws.[61] Among other things, it amended its extremely broad definition of what constituted a solicitation.[62] It used to require people to make qualifying statements even before a speech or an interview on the radio or television.

In a 2002 opinion, the U.S. Ninth Circuit Court found that even in the amended statute, "the Information Card endorsement requirement is a form of compelled speech that should have been subject to the same exacting scrutiny" that was applied in the *Riley* case.[63]

So why is the law still on the books, and why are charities still complying with it? According to sources in the legal community, it's because of an unwritten agreement between the city and its charities not to enforce the regulation. And because the sector has so few resources, an egregious violation of the humanitarian sector's First Amendment rights gets a pass because we can't afford do anything about it. So the city and its elected officials get to make a show to the general public of being appropriate watchdogs of the city's charities. Year after year, fundraising campaigns send the general public little slips of paper showing their previous year's overhead ratios, reinforcing in the public's mind that this is the information they should be most interested in.

A huge teachable moment is lost. We are statutorily institutionalizing bad civic education.

Other Examples of Bad Public Policy Abound

In another example, in May 2011 the state of Tennessee passed a law requiring that any charity, except "bona fide religious institutions" (apparently there's no concern that a church could ever waste charitable dollars), that receives more than twenty-five thousand dollars in donations connected with disaster relief must file quarterly financial reports with the secretary of state, "on forms prescribed by the secretary of state," specifying how much was raised and spent as a result of the solicitation.[64]

The prescribed form focuses exclusively on the typical administration-to-program ratio, requiring the charity to state gross revenues, program expenses, fundraising expenses, and administrative expenses.[65] This disaster relief requirement is in addition to existing Tennessee Department of State, Division of Charitable Solicitations and Gaming requirements that charities submit financial statements for the most recent fiscal year;[66] the requirement to file federal and state tax returns; the requirement to file a report with the institutional funder that may have provided a grant for their disaster relief efforts, postal regulations and laws governing the use of the nonprofit postal permits if they solicit by mail, and Federal Trade Commission and Federal Communications Commission rules regarding telemarketing if they use that method. And if they are involved in political activity, it is on top of Federal Election Commission rules.[67]

The state's Web site states:

> Learning about a charity before you donate can ensure that the organization to whom you donate is reputable, and that its mission matches your intentions. However, researching charities can be daunting. . . . [We] assist Tennesseans in this research process. The division maintains this information in a database, viewable to the public. Financial data includes revenues, expenses, and other changes to the balance sheet.

In fact it "assists" only if it is collecting and distributing truly meaningful information. To the extent it is not, it is doing damage.[68]

Just as I was about to put this chapter to bed, the Florida Senate Commerce and Tourism Committee approved a measure by a four-to-one vote that would cap salaries of charity leaders at $129,972 if the group receives more than two-thirds of its funding from the state. The move was prompted by reports of highly paid executives at some community-based care organizations, according to the *Jacksonville Business Journal*.[69]

What is an organization with a great leader it is paying $175,000 to do? Pass up the state funding or fire the leader?

There are far too many examples like this to list here.

These are the fundamental reasons we need a legal defense fund to deal with these issues.

First and foremost, we must recognize and combat the unintended consequences of each specific proposal and the harm they create for good organizations, on both a regulation-by-regulation basis and a collective basis.

Second, we ought not remain silent while the sector's free speech and commerce rights are trampled on, even as we fight for the constitutional rights of those we serve.

Third, we should not be simply reacting. We should have an entity with the resources to be proactively envisioning the long-term state and local regulatory environment in which we want to work.

Fourth, charities are not equipped to respond to attacks, which are a distraction from their critical work.

Fifth, we ought not to spend valuable resources reinventing the wheel of opposition each time measures like these are proposed. We should develop one national operation skilled in articulating the argument, well funded to advance it, and with the legal, political, and organizing proficiencies to defeat it.

Sixth, we could use each one of these battles as a teachable moment—for public officials, law enforcement, the media, the general public, and even members of our sector. (Unbelievab' the Nonprofit Association of Oregon found 87 percent of its members supporting the Oregon proposal.) Each case is an opportunity for us to be educating and learning. There was no national voice weighing in on the Oregon bill.

Seventh, we need to send a strong national message to state and local lawmakers that our sector will not be used as political red meat and that it will not be sacrificed on the altar of public opinion. ACFRFR recalls one case in which the California attorney general said in federal district court that he had advised the governor that a proposed regulation was unconstitutional but the governor had signed it anyway. Elected officials do this because they are so focused on popular opinion—and because they can get away with it.

Eighth, we lose when we are fragmented. Instead of restricting ourselves to the voices of those directly and immediately affected, we can bring to each battle voices from across the country. We are all adversely affected when these types of counterproductive ideas gather momentum. No locality should feel alone when challenged.

Ninth, we are all adversely affected by fraud in our sector, and current policies and resources don't do enough to target it. The Oregon proposal is one of many cases in which the criminal justice and law enforcement sectors use bulldozers where scalpels are required. Politically popular, ill-considered, throw-the-baby-out-with-the-bathwater solutions are proposed, often because of ignorance. Right now, policymakers are looking through a crimi- [illegible] lens at well-intended people working on difficult social [illegible] y are using measures like fundraising percentages [illegible] e and compare the difficulty and expense of raising [illegible] erent causes and organizations to form judgments [illegible] racter and intent of individuals. If their goal is truly to uncover fraud, they must come up with intelligent, investigative initiatives that accomplish that goal.

Finally, we must work to disassociate the public image of charities from law enforcement. Because many regulatory operations are aimed at fraud and housed in police departments, with gaming commissions, or in the offices of attorneys general, there is an immediate context of suspicion. Any organization that is required to file with law enforcement, which includes nearly all humanitarian organizations, is tainted by the association. Charities get conflated in people's minds with criminal activity and fraud. The preponderance of regulations that are proposed every year to combat fraud in charity only reinforces that effect.

If uncovering fraud is the goal, why single out charity in this way? Let's have fraud departments that include charity instead of charity departments looking for fraud. A 2004 Federal Trade Commission study on fraud in the United States lists the seven most common types of fraud: advance fee loans, buyers' clubs, credit card insurance, credit repair, prize promotions, Internet services, and pyramid schemes. Fraudulent charitable solicitations are not among them, despite the headlines they produce.

Next Steps

I have been in discussions with ACFRFR about a partnership with the Charity Defense Council wherein ACFRFR would contribute its considerable legal expertise in this arena and the Charity Defense Council would supply a larger infrastructure, database of supporters, and funding resources, and integrate its activities with the other programs of the council. This new entity would be tasked to do the following:

1. Create an online database of all existing federal, state, county, and local regulations. This will achieve three objectives. First, it will give us the first complete picture we've ever had of the regulatory lay of the land. Second, it will help organizations understand their existing statutory responsibilities at all levels. This will be of particular help to smaller organizations. Third, and most important, it will help us build the foundation for a comprehensive national, long-term strategy for dealing with regulation.
2. Create meaningful relationships with all states attorneys general. If these offices view us as a resource, they will consult with us prior to proposing regulation to gain from our legal expertise, learn about potential unintended consequences, and understand how the humanitarian sector will react to any proposal. If regulation is actually required, we can be of assistance in crafting it so that it doesn't produce unintended consequences and achieves its real objectives.
3. Create similar relationships with state legislators and their offices.
4. Reach out to newly elected public officials. In this way we can get people thinking proactively about things they can do to help the sector, rather than doing things that harm it in reaction to some future, unpredictable news event. In addition, we can let them know that they have a resource in us.
5. Create a task force to develop thoughtful methods and tactics for uncovering and dealing with fraud where it actually occurs and make our findings and ideas available to elected officials. This is desperately needed. If we are proactive about publicizing our own efforts at protecting the public interest, these efforts can only reflect well on us.

6. Coordinate with leaders outside the United States in order to understand the full scope of potential future regulation and provide technical assistance when some have experience in what others are encountering. That doesn't happen now.
7. Establish a hot line and coordinating office for dealing with unexpected regulations that do arise. This office would be the first point of contact for determining and organizing both initial response and ongoing strategy.
8. From a central place, develop political, legal, and public relations strategies for each battle we choose to engage, accumulating and employing institutional knowledge on each front.
9. Organize the sector on a national basis to come to the aid of peers facing onerous regulatory efforts in other state and local jurisdictions. If a local city manager gets nine hundred e-mails the day after a piece of bad policy is proposed, the outcry will not only serve notice of the error, but of the significance of the opposition the proposal will face. This database can also be engaged in the face of national regulatory efforts. It can be a force for vigilance on public policy at all levels of government.
10. Act as an advisory service to humanitarian organizations. The web of existing regulations is challenging to navigate. We can publish online tools that help humanitarian organizations understand them.
11. Build on the work of ACFRFR and eliminate regulation already on the books that is problematic or fails to serve the public interest.

This final task merits further discussion. Specifically, we must:

- Develop a strategy to stop government entities from discriminating against charitable organizations that don't meet certain overhead criteria. The U.S. Office of Management and Budget administers the combined federal campaign by which federal employees can make payroll deduction gifts to charities. It was previously sued by a charity that was deprived of the right to participate in the program based on a higher cost of fundraising ratio than the program specified as acceptable. The charity won based on long-standing U.S. Supreme Court precedent. As a result, the requirement was eliminated from the federal program. Despite this, many state and local government campaigns still use a minimum cost-of-fundraising ratio to exclude charities from participation in their charitable payroll deduction campaigns. If we had the resources, we could sue those governmental entities under the Civil Rights Act.

- Extend the gains achieved in the Pinellas cases on a circuit-by-circuit or, if necessary, state-by-state basis until there is no longer any registration requirement for out-of-state fundraising anywhere. This is critical for several reasons. First, these regulations don't just affect fundraising firms. They affect all of the humanitarian organizations those firms might work for: the breast cancer organizations we know and love, the organizations working on malaria, global poverty, the environment, domestic violence, and everything in between. Second, without fundraising for the cause, there is no cause. And third, this culture of regulation reinforces the public perception that charities waste money.
- Extend the principles set forth in the Pinellas cases to defeat overly burdensome registration regulations on charities. The cases were successful in forcing the county to significantly revise its registration requirements for charities. The litigation

took place under the U.S. Civil Rights Act (because it involved the First Amendment rights of charities as applied to the states under the Fourteenth Amendment, which addresses deprivation of rights under color of state law) and ACFRFR won attorneys' fees as well as injunctive relief.[70] That's an important fact going forward. With adequate resources, we could extend these kinds of actions against states that, for example, require fingerprinting or criminal background checks of charity officials or whose registrations are otherwise overly burdensome. Moreover, this would encourage states to focus their time, resources, and enforcement on real fraud rather than on the law-abiding charities that voluntarily register despite burdensome and expensive registration schemes.[71]

- Get regulations repealed that are currently on the books but unenforced by authorities because they are unconstitutional or otherwise unenforceable.
- Eliminate overly burdensome regulations on charities that solicit in states outside their primary place of business.
- Stop the Federal Trade Commission from unlawfully extending its jurisdiction to charitable organizations. Since the commission was founded, its jurisdiction has been "commerce among and between the states." The legislative history of the founding act makes it clear that its jurisdiction extends to interstate business commerce and not to nonprofit organizations. Yet periodically it seeks to extend its jurisdiction to hold sway over nonprofit organizations. This can create significant compliance expenses.[72]

Besides these unintended consequences, we must address registration regulations because they carry a heavy and often restrictive price tag. Geoffrey Peters has compiled the categories of direct, indirect, and opportunity costs of these requirements:

- *Fees to register as both a "charity" and a "foreign corporation."* Approximately forty states have their own solicitation registration requirements. Increasingly, states are requiring that charities register as "foreign corporations" in their state if they will be soliciting in that state, even though they may have no official presence there. Both of these requirements come with fees, and when they are multiplied by forty states, they add up.
- *Payments to registration professionals.* The state registration forms can be confusing. Their financial requests can vary widely, requiring charities to perform forty different accountings of the same financial data. Charities often end up hiring expensive legal and auditing counsel to make sure they don't run afoul of any state regulations.
- *Printing, stuffing, and mailing of mandatory disclosure statements.* On a per piece basis, this may cost only pennies. But pennies add up to thousands of dollars in printing and fulfillment costs when large organizations mail millions of solicitations.
- *Payments to accountants, auditors, and tax return preparers.* Accounting professionals have to be involved in the completion of registration and reporting forms, almost all of which demand financial information.
- *One-time or unusual costs associated with enforcement activities.* When the attorney general calls with an accusation or an inquiry, legal, finance, and administrative fees start to add up quickly, not to mention stresses on the organization.
- *Fundraiser compliance costs.* Fundraising firms have to pay registration fees in each state where registration is required. In many states, these firms have to obtain bonds valued in the

hundreds of thousands of dollars. Those bonds can cost as much as 5 to 6 percent of their value. Fundraising firms pass these costs along to the charities for which they are working.[73]

Aside from the costs associated with these requirements, they create a more damaging unintended effect: most of the organizations that are bearing those costs are fully complying with the laws. They're not the ones committing fraud—the ones the state should be looking for. It's the organizations that aren't complying, that aren't completing the forms, where real fraud is going on. Most states and municipal agencies lack the enforcement resources to fix that. So the net effect of all of this regulation is to lay unnecessary costs and distractions on the good guys.

In Conclusion

Bad regulation reinforces negative public perceptions about the humanitarian sector. How confusing it would be to run educational campaigns demonstrating to the public that overhead is an essential part of the cause, while their local attorney general is telling them that it's a statutory offense.

Vigilant attention to public policy must be part of any overarching effort to achieve the economic freedoms we require to create transformational change. If we're going to be subject to investigation for taking risks in fundraising that don't pan out, as risks have a tendency to do, or for running elevated levels of overhead for short periods of time in order to achieve tremendous scale in the long term, or for hiring a lead achieving Fortune 500 scale but who comes at prices, then we don't have economic freedom.

That goes to the heart of our cause.

5

Enact a National Civil Rights Act for Charity and Social Enterprise

All legislative Powers herein granted shall be vested in a Congress of the United States, which shall consist of a Senate and House of Representatives.

U.S. CONSTITUTION

It's 2015, and the National Civil Rights Act for Charity and Social Enterprise has just been enacted. It begins with a statement of purpose, inspired by the 1964 Civil Rights Act:

> To ensure the ability of tax-exempt organizations to realize their maximum potential to address issues of social concern, to create new corporate structures to maximize the ability of enterprising citizens to have a positive impact on the most urgent social issues of our time and to maximize the potential of public foundations and the citizenry to fund their efforts, to authorize the Attorney General to institute suits to protect the First Amendment rights of these individuals and organizations, to provide consistent standards throughout the nation for the conduct of and reporting on fundraising appeals, to allow tax-exempt organizations to conduct political advocacy without threat to their tax-exempt status,

> to provide the citizenry with consistent, up-to-date, comprehensive information on all of the nation's tax exempt organizations, and for other purposes.

Imagine that. Imagine if we actually addressed some of the statutory impediments to our ability to make progress.

Human beings have a profound propensity to suffer difficulties for long periods of time without realizing that there are productive things they can do about them. This tendency is pervasive in the humanitarian sector. We accept our difficulties. We don't think to fix them. We don't think to think that we could fix them. This acceptance is especially pronounced in our orientation toward the regulatory and statutory environment in which we work. Not only have we not fixed it to accommodate the needs of the modern era; we have not discussed or thought to discuss fixing it. So the hope of ever fixing it has been buried at least three levels below our consciousness.

When I began asking sector leaders about what points should go into a comprehensive piece of national legislation to advance the sector, I got responses like these:

"I am not very familiar with the legislation around charity."
"Neat idea."
"To be honest, we haven't been looking at this work through a legislative lens."
"[I] don't see any need for changes in federal regulations at this time."
"Nothing very interesting comes to my mind."

I built a Web site to collect ideas from people in the sector. I tweeted it to twenty-five hundred followers and posted three times on Facebook to a thousand friends. I got three legitimate responses, a .08 percent response. A normal direct mail response for just about anything is about 2 percent, or twenty-five times greater. So much for the value of social media. But what it really reflects is how utterly unconscious we are about the availability of public policy as a tool to improve our lot.

Most of us couldn't even begin to say what we would change. We couldn't even say what statutes and regulations we actually operate under. If put on the spot, we'd look like one of those sixteen-year-old kids when Jay Leno asks them to name the vice president of the United States.

Civil right activists and the Congress devised a sweeping set of national laws packaged in one breathtaking piece of legislation in 1964. The disabled community did the same thing in 1990 with the Americans with Disabilities Act. It's our time for a bold, forward-thinking, strategic, and comprehensive National Civil Rights Act for Charity and Social Enterprise. We can no longer live with a reactionary, fragmented set of laws and regulations designed, whether intentionally or unconsciously, to stand in our way.

One of the functions of the Charity Defense Council must be to develop a thoughtful process for the crafting of this legislation, collect the best thinking of leaders throughout the sector to guide it, and develop a mechanism and facility for that purpose.

This process should survey and consider needs and opportunities in all of the domains that intersect with our work on a day-to-day basis and over the long term:

- **Advocacy**—the rights and abilities of tax-exempt organizations in all classes to lobby their elected officials and effect political change.

- **Fundraising,** including attempts to restrict spending associated with it and onerous inconsistencies in state regulations associated with it.
- **Oversight authority,** including the rights and abilities of tax-exempt organizations and their boards to enter into contracts with individuals and third parties without second-guessing or the threat of interference from local, state, and federal government.
- **Corporate structures** that will allow financial incentive to help fuel productivity on urgent social issues.
- **Mergers and acquisitions** and the development of financial incentives to encourage them.
- **Federal and state contract requirements,** including reporting requirements and harmful restrictions on the amounts that tax-exempt organizations may or may not spend on their management and infrastructure.
- **Speech,** including protecting tax-exempt organizations from requirements that they speak in the language of overhead ratios or financial performance.
- **Civic philanthropy** and its expansion, including issues related to tax incentives.
- **Accounting standards and definitions,** including how tax-exempt organizations may or may not define their cause.
- **Institutional giving** and related opportunities and restrictions, including foundation-imposed reporting requirements on grantees and the ability of public foundations to fund for-profit social initiatives.
- **The Form 990.**
- **The Internal Revenue Service Tax Exempt Division** and its charter, capabilities, clarity of its regulations, ability to give quick guidance to individuals and organizations, and responsiveness to the sector.

- **Evaluation,** and the need for a comprehensive national charity database that includes every operating tax-exempt organization in the country and is accessible to everyone and easy to use.

I asked various leaders in the sector, the law, social enterprise, and the social capital movement what idea or ideas they thought ought to be contained in a sweeping national civil rights and social enterprise act. In this chapter, I lay out several of my own ideas first and then continue with the ideas contributed by others. This is the beginning of the conversation about the National Civil Rights Act for Charity and Social Enterprise.

Create a Corporate Structure for For-Profit Foundations

Right now, if you're an enterprising humanitarian with a great idea but you also have big dreams for your own economic future, you're out of luck. The only way you can put your idea in the marketplace is to structure your business as a 501(c)(3) tax-exempt organization. This means that, unlike the guys who started Ford Motor Company, Coca-Cola, and Apple, you can't own a penny of what you build. You can't offer any ownership interest to others who might want to build it with you. You can't put any of your own cash into it to get it started if you expect a financial return. You can't have job security either, because you have a board to report to that can decide at any time that your time is done. So you ask yourself, *Am I really willing to dedicate a huge chunk of my life—my best ideas, my heart and soul, and a bunch of my money—into something that I can never have any equity in and could be taken away from me at any time?*

Right now, such an entrepreneur could launch her idea as a for-profit corporation. But there are some big problems.

Let's say her idea is to launch a triathlon to find a cure for cancer. She calls the company Cancer Challenge, Inc. Each participant has to raise at least $3,000 for the charity in order to take part. She hopes to get a thousand participants and raise $3 million. She knows she'll have $1 million in hard costs—staff, promotion, logistics—and wants to keep $100,000 as profit. The remaining $1.9 million will go directly to a cancer charity to conduct research. She's not being greedy. By far the lion's share of what comes in—96 percent—is going directly to charity or the direct costs of the event. She's making a modest 4 percent profit. And to show its good faith, Cancer Challenge, Inc. makes its books completely open to the public, so everyone can see what's being spent on what in the same way they can with a charity.

Here are the problems with this scenario:

- The donors who contribute the $3 million cannot deduct the donations from their taxes because Cancer Challenge, Inc. is not tax exempt. It's for-profit. The current IRS definition of an *exempt purpose* requires that "none of [the organization's] earnings may inure to any private shareholder or individual."[1]
- People may not care about being unable to get a $5 tax savings on a $50 gift, but there's a real narrative problem. Imagine a participant saying to his best friend, "I want you to pledge me $100 for this charity event I am doing. Oh, but the donation is not tax deductible." It invites suspicion.
- Cancer Challenge, Inc. cannot deduct the $1.9 million it gives to charity from its taxes. Businesses can deduct gifts to charity only up to 10 percent of their total revenues. Cancer Challenge, Inc. had $3 million in revenues. It can deduct only $300,000 of the $1.9 million it gave to charity. It has to pay taxes, at probably a 33 percent rate, on $1.6 million of the

money it gave to charity—a whopping $528,000. It made only $100,000 in profit, so it can't cover the tax liability. And that's a tax liability that a foundation does not have because it's tax exempt. If every dollar donated to Cancer Challenge Inc. comes with a roughly 33 percent tax burden, who would want to give to it?

To avoid these pitfalls, our entrepreneur could set up Cancer Challenge, Inc. as a for-profit corporation, but instead of taking in the donations itself, donations would go directly to the cancer charity. Cancer Challenge, Inc. would sign a contract with the charity to produce the event on its behalf. The charity would pay Cancer Challenge, Inc. a fee for its services and would reimburse it for expenses out of the donation revenues the charity receives.

Here are the problems with this approach:

- All of the money Cancer Challenge, Inc. raises goes into someone else's bank account. What business would want all of its revenues deposited in someone else's account? What business that was making only a $100,000 profit would want to lay out $1 million for expenses on trust alone? And what bank is going to provide start-up financing for that kind of a business?
- The agreement with the charity will likely contain restrictions on the way Cancer Challenge, Inc. can spend money on the event. Imagine if Apple had to run its business and make spending decisions dictated by a third party that knows nothing about its business.
- Cancer Challenge, Inc. has to align its financial destiny with another entity that it knows little about and has no control over. The charity's culture may be different from Cancer Challenge, Inc.'s. It may undergo leadership changes that

dramatically affect Cancer Challenge, Inc. There are a hundred other unknowns.

As a last option, our entrepreneur could establish Cancer Challenge, Inc. as its own tax-exempt, nonprofit organization. Here are the problems with that:

- She can't own anything and can't offer others ownership.
- She can't be sure the board won't fire her, leaving her with nothing after building everything.
- The IRS may not grant tax-exempt status to Cancer Challenge, Inc. because, believe it or not, the IRS does not regard fundraising for charity as having a charitable purpose.

The solution is to create, through legislation, a for-profit foundation. This solves every problem and adds a world of great incentives. These are its features:

- It is a for-profit corporation. It can make profit, and it can sell and trade equity.
- It must establish that it has a charitable purpose.
- Fundraising for charities would be considered a charitable purpose.
- It must keep its books open to the public in the same way a charity must. The public can see how much profit the charity earns and what it pays its people. It can decide on its own if it believes the charity's expenses are prudent and its profit fair.
- Its tax forms are available to the public to examine at any time.
- It is not tax exempt. In other words, it has to pay taxes on its profits.
- It can deduct 100 percent of its gifts to charity from its taxes.

- Donations to the entity are fully tax deductible by the general public, as if they were giving to a charity, so long as the organization's activities are deemed to have a charitable purpose.
- Grants made to these corporations by public foundations count against the foundation's requirement to give away 5 percent of its assets each year.

These are the benefits of the for-profit foundation:

- We can drive a whole new class of entrepreneurial and creative thinking into civic philanthropy; we can drive new financially motivated capital into these ventures because equity can be sold.
- We can drive social benefit–motivated capital into these ventures because foundations will be able to make grants to them.
- We can increase civic philanthropy and finally start to move the needle up on that 2 percent of gross national product that is given to charity each year.

Some questions may arise:

Q: Why should it be tax exempt if it makes a profit?

A: It isn't tax exempt.

Q: Why should donors get a tax deduction if it is for-profit?

A: Because the donor is not getting any personal benefit. The entire donation is going into the organization's expenses, which are connected to producing a charitable benefit; or toward a charitable end purpose; or to profit, which will be taxed at the corporate rate. The current lack of tax deductibility is irrational. The reason I get a tax deduction for giving to a nonprofit homeless shelter is that I'm trying to accomplish some social good and there's no material gain for me. The moment I receive any material gain, like a chicken dinner at a charity event, I can't deduct that portion of my donation.

Q: What about salaries? Why should contributions to those be tax deductible?

A: Again, if the organization has a charitable purpose, its leaders' salaries contribute to the production of charitable results, and the government gets its share because the salaries are taxed at ordinary income rates.

Q: Who determines how much profit is too much?

A: The market does. If the market determines that Cancer Challenge, Inc. is charging too much profit, it stops donating to it. This is a built-in incentive for the corporation to be reasonable.

Use the Corporate Structure to Create For-Profit Charities

This idea of a for-profit foundation can be extended to corporations that want to provide direct services. In the example of Cancer Challenge, Inc., the social profit, so to speak—$1.9 million—is being given to a cancer research charity as a grant. But there's no reason the social profit couldn't stay within the organization to allow the organization to provide the services itself. All kinds of businesses could arise if social entrepreneurs were supported by the tax code in this way—for example, a for-profit homeless shelter, an anti–gang violence project, a Parkinson's disease research lab, or any other venture that's working to produce positive social transformation.

What an incredible marketplace of ideas and energy this would create. And the financial incentive would increase competition in the best possible way. These corporations would have to show consumers that they are committed to having an impact in order to establish a competitive advantage over their peers. And in cases where competition is not effective for solving the problem, the companies that could work together best would prosper together. There might even be incentives to merge.

Change IRS Regulations to Define Fundraising as Having a Charitable Purpose

Currently, for a corporation to gain 501(c)(3) tax-exempt status with the IRS, it must have a charitable, or "exempt," purpose, as follows:

> The exempt purposes set forth in section 501(c)(3) are charitable, religious, educational, scientific, literary, testing for public safety, fostering national or international amateur sports competition, and preventing cruelty to children or animals. The term *charitable* is used in its generally accepted legal sense and includes relief of the poor, the distressed, or the underprivileged; advancement of religion; advancement of education or science; erecting or maintaining public buildings, monuments, or works; lessening the burdens of government; lessening neighborhood tensions; eliminating prejudice and discrimination; defending human and civil rights secured by law; and combating community deterioration and juvenile delinquency.

The definition does not include fundraising. So while relief of the poor is considered to be charitable, raising money to increase the amount of relief to the poor is not. The advancement of education is considered charitable, but fundraising to advance the advancement of education is not.

So as I stated in the example above, if our entrepreneur wanted to establish Cancer Challenge, Inc. as a nonprofit tax-exempt organization, she likely would not be able to get the IRS to grant her tax-exempt status.

The fact that fundraising is not considered to have a charitable purpose in and of itself is indicative of our deeply flawed perspective on fundraising.

Current definitions are illogical for two reasons. First, virtually every tax-exempt organization engages in fundraising activities. The contributions that go to those organizations, including the portion that goes to the organization's fundraising efforts, are fully tax deductible. The revenue that those organizations take in and expend on fundraising is tax exempt. If we really don't regard fundraising for charity as having a charitable purpose, then we shouldn't allow the portion of donations that supports fundraising to be tax deductible or the portion of income that an organization spends on fundraising to be tax exempt. Indeed, under current definitions, a donor who wants to make a targeted gift to support the hiring of a new fundraising officer at his favorite charity should not be able to deduct any of the gift, and the charity should have to pay taxes on that person's entire gift. But this is not what actually happens. So clearly we do believe that fundraising has a charitable purpose. Indeed, the IRS believes it and practices that belief.

Second, the notion that fundraising for charity doesn't have a charitable purpose is irrational on its face. Without fundraising, the organization would not be able to fulfill any charitable purpose, so it is axiomatic that the purpose of fundraising is charitable.

By defining fundraising as having a charitable purpose, we can open up the doors of a corporate structure to those whose expertise is in fundraising and who want to establish fundraising-specific, tax-exempt organizations. We can also f opment of core expertise within these organizat not the best idea for every charity in America t expert on, for example, event production. Mayb have a few large organizations that hone their skil... in that area and relieve service providers of having to dedicate critical internal resources to that effort. In addition, larger fundraising organizations can develop economies of scale that fragmented fundraising operations cannot.

Fund an iTunes for Charity

Imagine this: you log onto Everycharity.org, and the site is as visually seductive as iTunes. It most definitely does not look as if it was designed by a Ph.D. candidate in accounting. The icons look so good you want to lick them, as Steve Jobs once remarked about the icons in the Mac operating system. Instead of reading like it was written by a committee of academics, it's as easy to understand as Mr. Rogers. Instead of being filled with acronyms and social service jargon, it contains words that anyone can understand. The words actually inspire you instead of confusing you. Instead of intimidating, it invites. Instead of frustrating you, it fills you with a sense of possibility.

On the home page is a giant heart where you type in the name of the charity you want to learn about. It's a new organization, so you're expecting an error message: "Not found." But the organization is actually there! A video pops up with a big Play button. You watch the executive director of the charity talk for five minutes about the organization's goals, the progress it's making—or not making—toward those goals, and what information the organization uses to gauge its results.

There's another big button, this one labeled Results. It leads to a jargon-free summary—written by people who spent time meeting with the organization's staff, clients, and constituents—that describes what the organization has been up to over the past year, the results it has achieved or tried to achieve, its strengths, and what its weaknesses appear to be.

Who are these people who visit the organizations, examining their goals, creating the videos, and writing the summaries? They're trained professionals, graduate students, and recent college graduates, all part of the Cause Corps—a kind of Peace Corps for evaluating the work of charities. These superskilled, conscientious, and objective analysts visit every operating charity in America to do annual surveys. If the charity is very small, Cause Corps members might spend only a day or two. For a larger organization, they might spend a week. Every active charity gets a visit—all 700,000 or so of them—every year. Not one is left out, and every profile is fresh, up-to-date, and objective.

Why every charity? Because the site won't get widespread use if people know they can't find the charity they're looking for. Some people might say that only the large, established charities should be considered. But the small upstarts might very well be doing the best work, and donors should know that.

You can find other information on the site too: for instance, a user-friendly analysis of how the organization scored on an "intention-to-do-good" test, similar to what the folks at the Commonwealth Market, an organization looking at new ways of getting at the soul of an organization, have built. Does the charity have goals? Does everyone in the organization know what they are? Are they collecting data to measure their progress? Do the data have integrity? Do they analyze the data? Do they change their behavior based on what the data teach them?

A big Innovation button would link to information about how innovative the organization is—how its approach differs from traditional approaches and what's different about the way the organization is attacking the problem.

And if you don't know what charity you want to explore, you can browse by cause. Just the way iTunes introduces you to great artists you may never have heard of, we could motivate donors to place interesting bets on cool organizations that were previously unknown to them.

Financial data are also featured prominently. The Web site could draw tax information from GuideStar, but instead of rendering it in the form of intimidating charts, it would create three-dimensional bar graphs and colorful pie charts, beautifully lit, and in the colors of candy. Maybe the pie charts are actually pictures of, well, pie, so people actually want to look at them.

If the charity has also been reviewed by an evaluator like the Better Business Bureau's Wise Giving Alliance, GiveWell (it does its own research on about five hundred charities), GreatNonprofits (it assembles donor feedback), Philanthropedia (it gathers expert opinion on about two hundred humanitarian organizations), or Charity Navigator (it has financial information on about seven thousand charities), then that information would be there to look at as well.

Some people will say that the public doesn't want any of this. They just want a letter grade—something quick and simple. Ten years ago, the public didn't want MP3 players. Why? Because no one knew what on earth an MP3 player was, and even the name was intimidating. *iPod*, on the other hand, sounds friendly. People don't know what they want until someone offers it to them in an accessible and inspirational way.

How much would this cost? With a generous margin of error, I'd say about $1.5 billion annually. Assuming a management and general cost of 30 percent of that total, $1.03 billion would be left for assessment. This figure is commensurate with meaningful investigations. If the agency's analysts were paid $65,000 annualized ($1,250 weekly, or $31.25 hourly) and assuming there are 700,000 active charities in the nation, the funds would provide enough resources for about forty-seven hours of investigation and summary for each charity per year.

A billion and a half dollars sounds huge—but not when you realize that it represents about one-half of 1 percent of what Americans donate to charity each year. Then it sounds like the minimum amount we ought to be spending to monitor and evaluate all of this giving in a way that's consistent across the board. Everyone could use the information—individuals, state attorneys general, foundations, the media, other charities—and everyone would operate with the same objective baseline data.

Perhaps this sounds crazy, but the best ideas in history sound crazy when they're new. Think of when Henry Ford proposed the automobile, with the resulting need to build millions of miles of asphalt roads, with street lights and traffic lights at every intersection, and a million gas stations to fill the cars with fuel. Or when Edison said you'd need to run millions of miles of poles and wire all over the country, to every single house, in order to make the light bulb work.

Funding for this resource should begin with the federal government. The act should include a mechanism by which, over time, humanitarian organizations pay into a fund to operate the system on a sliding scale based on their revenues. Once funded and on its feet, it could transition into a tax-exempt effort run by leaders elected by the humanitarian organizations themselves.

The effort should include a marketing budget on the order of $100 million annually for at least five years in order to educate the general public about the existence of this invaluable new tool.

Visions from Visionaries

Those are a few of my ideas. Here are some of the ideas others have submitted.

1. Allow Private Foundations to Lobby on the Same Terms as Their Grantees, by Lawrence Mendenhall, Vice President, General Counsel, and Secretary, Humanity United

One of the most striking developments in the charitable sector over the past two decades is the rise in private foundation funding for public policy advocacy. This development reflects a growing recognition that some of the most pressing issues confronting our world today—from climate change to nuclear proliferation to food safety—cannot be solved by traditional grant making.

The challenge, however, is that private foundations are not permitted to lobby on legislative issues. The federal tax laws forbid it. Earmarking private foundation grants for legislative lobbying is also prohibited. The penalties for breaking the law, although rarely, if ever, imposed, are stiff and even extend to personal liability for foundation managers. Confusingly, public charities—the organizations that are most likely to receive foundation grants—can lobby for legislation, within limits imposed by the IRS, and can even use private foundation funds for legislative lobbying, so long as the foundation and its grantees are clever enough to exploit certain loopholes in the tax code. (Note that for-profit entities are not subject to limitations on legislative lobbying, which means that the for-profit perspective often dominates the legislative policy debate.)

This two-tier system, in which foundations cannot lobby legislatively but their public charity grantees can, creates the need for private foundations with legislative policy goals to employ armies of lawyers and accountants to help ensure compliance with the letter, if not the spirit, of the no-lobbying law. While many of the larger foundations are willing to take on this added expense, the law deters many smaller foundations from funding any type of public policy advocacy at all, even nonlegislative advocacy.

The solution is to permit private foundations to lobby for legislation and fund legislative lobbying on the same terms as their public charity grantees. Like public charities, private foundations would be required to publicly report the amount of their legislative lobbying, and a private foundation's lobbying expenditures could not be "substantial" (the limit that applies to legislative lobbying by public charities). Overall, private foundation support for legislative lobbying would become more transparent, and private foundations would be more likely to invest in legislative lobbying efforts that would advance their charitable goals. The result would be greater charitable impact at virtually no cost. Since the IRS rarely imposes penalties on private foundations for legislative lobbying, changing the rules to permit them to lobby legislatively will have a negligible impact on revenues.

2. Build Philanthropic Equity into America's Nonprofit Accounting Rules, by George Overholser, Cofounder, Third Sector Capital Partners

Everybody knows you can't own a nonprofit. This is why, in some smoke-filled room in the 1950s, the concept of nonprofit equity was excluded from the rules of nonprofit accounting. It may have seemed like a good idea at the time, but what a huge mistake!

Here's an example of why. Several years ago, I had two meetings that taught me what happens when a nonprofit has no true equity. The first meeting was with a for-profit that had just received a significant amount of new equity. Of course, even though it now had growth capital in hand, its revenues were still zero. This is because equity accounting does not classify its $5 million equity check as "revenue" (the revenue label is strictly reserved for money received in exchange for products and services). These accounting rules for equity make a lot of sense. It would have been misleading to show revenues of $5 million for a company that hadn't yet figured out how to attract customers to buy its products.

My second meeting was with a nonprofit that had also just received a big dose of growth capital from philanthropic investors. Following nonprofit accounting rules, the nonprofit was required to classify every penny of growth capital as revenues—precisely the opposite of how for-profit accounting treats growth capital.

Why does this matter? Consider what happened next.

First, the nonprofit's executive director decided to dismantle the ongoing fundraising operation. Second, the philanthropic investors quickly realized that they had created what was rapidly beginning to look like a dependency relationship. And third, having learned that big checks breed dependency, the investors (rationally) decided never to write a big check again unless it was for something tangible, permanent, and with a known price tag—like a building or an endowment.

This would all be fine, except that growth capital simply doesn't work unless the checks are big. If the growth capital checks are small, management spends most of its time chasing growth capital and never gets around to building the type of organization that knows how to attract reliable, sustainable flows of revenues—money, that is, in exchange for products and services.

A typical venture-backed for-profit enterprise might take on $10 million of equity growth capital from four or five investors and then draw down those monies for the next five years as it learns how to sell 10 million widgets a year to customers for a buck a piece. Not so for nonprofits. For the vast majority of them, there simply is no such thing as upfront growth capital. More often than not, they are doomed to a month-to-month fundraising existence from which they never emerge.

In truth, nonprofits need equity accounting just as much as for-profits do. Without "equity," the distinction is lost between building a nonprofit (that's what equity is used for) and paying a nonprofit for its activities (that's what revenues are supposed to do). In nonprofit accounting, no one can tell the difference between money that is one-time growth capital and money that is part of ongoing revenue. And so philanthropists who are interested in firm building can't answer questions like these: How much did it cost to build this nonprofit? How do I know when we are done building so I can stop writing these huge checks?

In short, a major reason we don't have a market for nonprofit growth capital is that our accounting rules leave growth capital investors absolutely blind as to whether their investments worked.

The problem is easily solved. For starters, nonprofit equity requires no formal ownership rights. I know this is true, because I have built two nonprofit firms—NFF Capital Partners, a division of Nonprofit Finance Fund, and Third Sector Capital Partners—that offered workarounds that "tricked" nonprofit accounting (without conveying any ownership, or siphoning off any profits!) into demonstrating something that looks an awful lot like equity. Philanthropists love the concept because, like buildings and endowments, the equity concept puts a limited price tag on something tangible and permanent that they can point to. Indeed, over the course of four years, our sixteen clients at NFF were able to raise close to $400 million of highly flexible philanthropic equity.

Now it is time to make this innovation available to all nonprofits. There is no good reason that philanthropic equity cannot be inserted into America's accounting rules, so that thousands of deserving nonprofits can at last attract the growth capital they need and report it effectively as they build sustainable organizations.

3. Establish a New National Estimate of Charitable Impact, by Bill Shore, Founder, Share Our Strength

There are a lot of things the federal government could and should do to empower the nonprofit sector to achieve greater impact, but economic and political realities dictate that precious few of them are going to happen anytime soon. There is one step, however, that could be taken immediately, wouldn't have any significant cost associated with it, but could nevertheless have a huge impact on how the public perceives the sector and the degree to which it is willing to accord it the respect, investment, and professional support it deserves.

The Treasury Department and the Congressional Budget Office should publish an annual national estimate of charitable impact on taxpayers that sets out how much money the nonprofit sector has saved the American taxpayer, in total and per person. As federal and state governments have cut back in the wake of huge deficits and taxpayer revolts, especially in education, health care, workforce development, and antipoverty work, a wide range of national, regional, and community-based organizations have tried to pick up the slack, every year facing the challenge of having to do more with less. For most of the public, this is work being done somewhere else for someone else, with little recognition of just how directly it affects both the larger common good and their own wallet.

This estimate is different from simply the amount of money that is donated or spent by charitable organizations. It ought to take into account the direct cost savings from the countless human and social services that community-based nonprofits provide and government no longer pays for. It should also take into account projections of future savings likely to result from the investments in preventive measures that in the classic "ounce of prevention, pound of cure" sense save billions of tax dollars in future costs associated with health, remedial education, juvenile justice, and other needs.

The new national estimate is more than just a nice-to-know statistic. It goes directly to quantifying one aspect of the indispensable role played by nonprofits that necessitates their need to invest in themselves, take risks, pay competitive compensation, advertise, and compete for supporters. Too many Americans assume that nonprofits do important but small things. The national estimate would be at least one way to quantify how those small things add up to something really big and how they have an impact on each and every one of us.

4. Helping Nonprofit Health and Human Service Providers Cover Delayed Government Reimbursements, by Diana Aviv, President and CEO, Independent Sector

Critical infrastructure across our nation is crumbling, but I'm not referring to disintegrating roads, leaky dams, or unsafe bridges. This infrastructure involves nonprofit organizations, contracted by federal, state, and local governments to provide ential services such as food banks, homeless shelters, and are. Many of these services have already been elimi- scaled back, and many more operate at great risk, due to delayed reimbursements, funding cuts, and contract changes. A low- or no-interest bridge loan program would shore up the vital infrastructure that provides lifeline services to people suffering deep economic hardship.

It's no secret that federal, state, and local government coffers are badly depleted. The Center on Budget and Policy Priorities found that since 2008, forty-six states have cut funding across the board. Thirty-one states have trimmed health care programs, and twenty-nine slashed care for elderly and disabled people.[2] Many have cut programs or altered their contracts with health and human services providers at a time when demand for services is sky high.

A hard-hitting recession and sluggish recovery have left 46.2 million people in poverty, including 22 percent of our children, the worst statistics recorded since 1993.[3] Census data show record numbers sliding into deep poverty, defined as those with incomes at or below 50 percent of the poverty level (eleven thousand dollars for a family of four).[4]

Nonprofit health and human services providers lessen such hardship, but their services are possible only with significant funding from public resources. In 2010, the government issued some 200,000 contracts and grants to 33,000 health and human services providers; for the majority, the government is their largest source of revenue.[5] Yet in the past few years, these contracts have not been honored in a timely way. A study by the Urban Institute concluded that over half reported receiving late payments, and nearly 60 percent reported the government changing their contract or grant *after* services had been rendered.[6]

A bridge loan could alleviate the heavy burden placed on nonprofits by delayed government reimbursements. How would it work? The federal government could enlist community banks and other financial institutions to offer no- or low-interest loans to nonprofits. Under this approach, nonprofit groups would be able to use accounts receivables (essentially government IOUs) as collateral for temporary, short-term loans.

A bridge loan would offer health and human services agencies the capital they need to cover delayed reimbursements and would be a far less expensive fix than allowing programs to falter or be cut altogether. Such loans would be low-risk ventures to a cash-strapped government. Over the past forty years, 96 percent of loans made to nonprofits had been fully repaid with interest, according to FSG social impact advisors.[7] When government assets begin to replenish, loans could be rolled back as needed.

The benefits of a bridge loan outweigh the costs. Adopting this program would stabilize our nation's infrastructure of health and human services providers and, more important, ameliorate suffering and hardship for millions of people.

5. Require a Three-Year Progress Report for New Tax-Exempt Organizations, by Bob Ottenhoff, President and CEO, GuideStar

One of the defining characteristics of the nonprofit sector is the relatively low barrier for starting a new nonprofit organization. Any individual with a strong dose of passion and a little initiative can organize a new nonprofit organization and receive IRS authorization. This fits the American character. Americans, by nature, are inclined to take action when there's a job to be done, and they do not wait for someone else or the government to take it on. As a result, tens of thousands of new nonprofits are formed each year, usually led by a determined entrepreneur and often supported by eager donors and ambitious volunteers. These new organizations frequently are incubators for innovation, trying new approaches that sometimes help change the face of philanthropy. Along the way, thousands of new jobs are created. This spirit of innovation and entrepreneurship is good for the nonprofit sector and good for the American economy.

But what happens when a great idea doesn't work out or the passion of the moment begins to fade as the crisis is no longer front and center? In the for-profit world, a start-up entrepreneur has two stark choices: go out of business or sell the enterprise. In the nonprofit world, entrepreneurs have numerous ways to attract donor funding and keep the doors open. It takes only a good grant proposal or an emotional fundraising appeal to raise just enough money. But often it's just enough money to keep the doors open, though not enough to succeed and certainly not enough to become a high-performing organization. Today hundreds of thousands of nonprofit organizations are performing below minimum standards.

I propose that the Internal Revenue Service add a new detail before it grants authorization for a new nonprofit organization: a requirement to file a status report after three years of operation that focuses on impact. In this new report, the organization would answer three simple but profound questions: What is the mission of my organization? What are we doing to reach that mission? How are we measuring our progress?

The document would be posted on the IRS Web site and be made publicly available on sites such as GuideStar. The status report would help donors make better and more confident decisions about which organizations to support (or not). It would begin to expose those that are abusing the sector and perhaps help eager innovators think twice about starting another new organization. Most important, it would help to underscore the fact that it's not starting the organization that matters. It's certainly not about overhead ratios or how hard someone works. What really matters is how a nonprofit is making a difference and creating impact.

6. Set New Standards for Qualifying for Tax-Exempt Status, by Errol Copilevitz, Senior Partner, Copilevitz & Canter

There is a low entry barrier to obtaining tax-exempt status. With the help of competent legal counsel, one can file an IRS Form 1023 (a complicated business plan) and most likely be granted the privilege of operating a tax-exempt organization. The IRS does not delve into the history of the applicant.

Our firm has seen in its practice a wide range of applicants. While most have good intentions, unfortunately some possess few qualifications, and, in some instances, improper motivation.

Many professions require licensing, and in some instances, there is a continuing professional education requirement. Our firm believes that the charitable community would be more effective if the requirements for initiation of tax-exempt status were strengthened: by instituting a mandate that applicants without significant past experience who seek to start new charitable organizations be required to complete a minimum number of hours of instruction on management, fundraising, and professionalism.

This continuing education requirement could be satisfied through courses at colleges or universities (some of which already provide courses on nonprofit management) or by accredited trade associations. The IRS could sponsor annual symposiums in major markets featuring representatives of the agency, along with invited outside professionals.

The chief executive officer of a new charity could apply for an exemption from this requirement if he or she has a specific amount of past experience in the industry. The tax-exempt status granted to a new applicant would be a conditional grant subject to revocation for failing to take a predetermined number of courses in the first year of operation. These same standards could be imposed on any new CEO who comes to the position without the requisite amount of experience in the industry. Failure to take the necessary courses would disqualify the individual from acting as a CEO.

Introducing a new level of professionalism into the charitable community will engender a higher degree of confidence in the donating public and the regulatory community. Charitable dollars are too precious to be wasted in the hands of inefficient organizations.

The next step would be to introduce mandatory training for those who serve on boards of directors of tax-exempt organizations.

7. Support Nonprofit Collaborations and Mergers: The Catalyst Fund for Nonprofits, by Paul Grogan, President and CEO, and Jennifer Aronson, Director of Nonprofit Effectiveness, the Boston Foundation

Author's note: Grogan and Aronson write here about a successful experiment they are conducting at the Boston Foundation that encourages more collaboration, even mergers, of humanitarian organizations. This is a critical issue if we are to increase our chances of solving social problems. The legislative outcomes of this work could include establishing a fund to provide technical assistance and creating a mechanism—perhaps in the form of tax credits—for incentivizing more merger activity.

If you are reading this, chances are that you share both the desire to improve our communities and the knowledge that our challenges are immense, and that it will take all of us working together to effect real change. It is in this spirit that we see the Boston Foundation not as an end in and of itself, but as a means to an end—to strengthen our city and region and to increase opportunity for everyone. This is also one of the core principles on which the Catalyst Fund for Nonprofits was founded.

One of the key findings from the Boston Foundation's June 2008 report, "Passion & Purpose: Raising the Fiscal Fitness Bar for Massachusetts Nonprofits," was the mismatch that exists between the number of nonprofit organizations working in our communities and the financial resources that are available to support them. While many in the sector bristled initially at the idea of consolidation as a potential solution, the subsequent onset of the global financial crises, and the harsh reality of reduced government funding for nonprofits, resulted in an openness on the part of many organizations to explore new ways of doing business, including collaborative ventures and mergers.

Although a robust infrastructure exists in the corporate world to facilitate and support mergers and acquisitions, analogous expertise and resources have traditionally been difficult to identify and access in the nonprofit sector. Buoyed by recommendations that came out of a national roundtable discussion on nonprofit collaboration that we co-convened in 2009, the Boston Foundation launched the five-year, $1.725 million Catalyst Fund for Nonprofits in partnership with local funders Boston LISC, the Hyams Foundation, and the United Way of Massachusetts Bay and Merrimack Valley, and we recently welcomed the Kresge Foundation, our first national partner, which brings the fund up to $1.925 million.

By providing both financial support and access to vetted technical expertise, the Catalyst Fund models a resource infrastructure to facilitate strategic nonprofit collaboration. As a funder collaborative, the Catalyst Fund also fulfills the critical function of normalizing dialogue between nonprofits and funders on this previously taboo topic. Strategic collaboration between and among nonprofit organizations can include a spectrum of activities ranging from back-office resource sharing to a full merger. In selecting collaborations to support, the Catalyst Fund looks for collaborations that (1) preserve, expand, or improve the delivery of services; (2) meaningfully change the way participating organizations do business for the long term; and (3) demonstrate the commitment of the organizations' boards of directors. As in the for-profit sector, the purpose of this work is not always to rescue struggling organizations but rather to strengthen the impact of critical organizations in the communities they serve.

In its first year, the Catalyst Fund made investments in nine promising collaborations that include twenty-three organizations, and we are now beginning to see the ventures making progress toward their goals. These upfront investments in strategic collaborations are not quick fixes, but instead are focused on long-term viability and improving the impact of programs and services. Though the idea is still too often received with skepticism by nonprofit leaders, collaborations, including mergers, are a necessary and critical strategy to strengthen the nonprofit sector and improve our communities. Growth and replication of the Catalyst Fund model, informed by best practices and data-driven outcomes, will be an important tool to maximize the effectiveness, health, and ultimately the impact of nonprofit organizations for the long term.

8. Establish a Public-Private Partnership to Methodically Improve Charities' Effectiveness, by Eric Walker, Cofounder, InsideNGO

1. Nonprofits suffer from a conundrum. Donors typically want them to be efficient and effective, in that order. "Efficient" means delivering programs at the lowest practical cost, especially the lowest possible overhead cost. Yet donors are clamoring for results and impact, which require resources to be deployed effectively—meaning not necessarily at the lowest possible cost. Often donors are willing to fund the direct project costs required to meet effectiveness

sures, but they have little interest in moving beyond iency into funding overhead costs. The donor's percep- often is that if too many funds are dedicated to overhead functions, less will be available for the program. The missing link is the need for the concurrent goals of effectiveness in overhead functions, along with effectiveness in the program.

2. What do effective overhead services look like? If we take the major competencies as found, for example, in the McKinsey Capacity Assessment Grid, norms can be established for effectiveness for those areas in or supported by overhead. A test against the norms will reveal what an NPO does well and where investment is needed. Targeted investments are needed over and above current levels of overhead cost recovery. Those in need should be eligible for more funding upfront, in addition to the donor-prescribed rate. Effectiveness should be funded first.
3. The mind-set of the donor community needs to change from overhead efficiency and program effectiveness to overall organizational effectiveness and program results being pursued at the same time.
4. A legislative act should include a section to set up a public-private partnership of private foundations, nonprofits, government, and consulting firms for the purpose of leveraging resources to methodically improve charitable organization effectiveness over time. Key parameters could include:
   - Private foundations willing to pledge 1 percent of their annual payout to charitable organization effectiveness grants (OEGs) would receive a reduction in their IRS payout requirements in an amount equal to two times the amount of grants made within the payout testing period.
   - Private foundations that award OEGs at or above their 1 percent pledge and implement OEG common standards (for example, allowing total direct costs to be the base

for computing the grant overhead percentage) would be eligible to use an effective grant maker mark on all materials.

- Nonprofits willing to submit to an effectiveness capacity assessment and willing to commit to a three-year effectiveness-improvement plan would be eligible for OEGs in those areas showing need for improvement.
- Consulting firms would offer pro bono services for OEG assessments and provide OEG services at cost when funded by a qualifying grant, allowing them to use an effectiveness provider mark on all services and count pro bono services and rate discounts as charitable contribution deductions.

5. The federal government would amend IRS private foundation rules to allow the payout multiplier effect described in item 1 in this list and for an increase in the charitable contribution tax deduction described in item 4.

9. A Public Money Pathway, by John Tyler, General Counsel, Kauffman Foundation

There is such continuing clamor about philanthropic assets being "public money" that it seemed worthwhile to wonder how that assertion might play out logically if true. One likely scenario is a radically altered charitable sector and a vulnerable business sector.

If philanthropic assets are "public money," then what prevents the entities that hold such assets from merely being agents of government? If they are agents of government, then government officials—elected, appointed, or hired—dictate their missions, strategies, allocations, expenditures, governance, and more.

If philanthropic agents are subject to dictates of government officials, particularly those beholden to popularity, then what prevents their usurpation or elimination of those whose purposes are no longer in favor? And what prevents these enterprises from becoming patronage spoils for political victors to determine where such dollars are spent and how much?

If these dollars are a patronage prize, then nothing distinguishes philanthropic assets from actual tax revenues, except for the false pretenses under which the giving of those assets was enticed.

With that, we arrive back where we began: with philanthropic assets being public money, except there is a lack of freedom, independence, autonomy, privacy, or vibrancy that currently invigorates the sector. Moreover, with little or nothing left to differentiate the charitable sector from government, there may be consequences for constitutional freedoms of speech, association, possibly religion, and even contract. In effect, the sector disappears.

That, however, is not where the journey necessarily ends.

We then should wonder about the basis for asserting that philanthropic assets are public money in the first place, the most common of which relies on tax exemptions, deductions, and credits. Of course, tax-favored treatment is not limited to the charitable sector such that if tax treatment alone can justify declaring philanthropic assets as public, then it can also justify treating for-profit and individual assets as public. Tax treatment then becomes the basis for government interference in operations, governance, and decision making of business and privacy rights of individuals, particularly if views are unpopular.

Active efforts based on the "public money" misnomer at federal and state levels and within executive and legislative branches suggest that we ignore the above scenarios at our peril. The charitable sector and its contributions merit ongoing vigilance, including against those who would abuse or misuse it. Surely there are principled boundaries to prevent the above outcomes. Given the important roles that the sector fulfills, there must be an evergreen discipline of enduring principles that protect it.

Principled policy solutions could supplement vigilance through legislation or judicial opinions, or both, that unambiguously affirm that philanthropic assets are not literally public money and condemn attempts to impose obligations or proscriptions on that basis. Policy solutions, however, cannot substitute for relentless efforts to defend sector independence from debilitating threats and to ensure that the sector continuously validates the value of its autonomy and the underlying trust on which it is based.

Fortunately, sound, reasoned thinking has so far prevailed. We must make certain that it continues to do so.

10. Overarching Legislative Solutions to Problems of State and Local Charity Regulation, by Geoffrey Peters, President, American Charities for Reasonable Fundraising Regulation

Author's note: Peters looks at four problems related to overzealous regulation of charities. Significantly, none has a federal legislative solution.

The most popular solution [to overzealous state and local regulation] is also the most dangerous: federal preemption. Congress could attempt to give exclusive federal jurisdiction to the Federal Trade Commission (FTC), based on interstate commerce, to regulate charities and thus remove that regulation from the purview of the states. This would be difficult to achieve since charities are organizationally creatures of state, not federal, law. They are associations, corporations, or trusts—all created under state law. It is also politically unlikely that this would happen. Powerful state politicians would persuade powerful federal legislators to share power. It is more likely that we'd end up with concurrent jurisdiction and, in the process, cede the idea that the FTC has no jurisdiction over nonprofits. Even if we somehow secured exclusive federal jurisdiction, it would merely take the political appointment of the wrong federal charity czar to severely inhibit or destroy the opportunity for new ideas and new charities to survive or thrive. At least with state regulation, you have fifty chances of someone getting it right. With exclusive federal jurisdiction, getting it wrong means the death penalty.

The solution to [multitudes of concurrent and overlapping and conflicting local regulations] is simple and straightforward: convince the states to pass legislation stipulating that regulation of charities is exclusively the purview of state law. Some states already have this. Do not enable home-rule cities and counties to regulate charities because often such regulation is duplicative of state regulation, is burdensome and expensive, and accomplishes no greater consumer protection than any such protection afforded by the state. The only drawback is the need to lobby for this in states where it isn't already the law.

This problem [of using fundraising ratios or other faulty measures to regulate charities] has been "solved" at the federal, state, and local governmental levels by the U.S. Supreme Court. The law is clear. The problem is that not everyone follows it. Therefore, the solution is litigation wherever the law is being ignored: "Those who expect to reap the blessings of freedom must . . . undergo the fatigue of supporting it," wrote Thomas Paine in *The American Crisis* in 1777.

Ever since Hubert Humphrey ran for the Senate from Minnesota by claiming that as state attorney general he cleaned up charity fraud and abuse, politicians have known that they can get headlines by "exposing charitable fraud and abuse." The acronym NAAG (National Association of Attorneys General) is often referred to sardonically as "National Association of Aspiring Governors." In one well-known instance, a politician running for governor took twelve supposedly faulty and incomplete applications for state registration and held a press conference warning the public not to contribute to these twelve scofflaw organizations. The press conference made the TV and page one news. One day later, the twelve charities revealed that all had properly filed answers to questions they'd been asked, and the response mail was hung up in another unit of the charity registration bureau. All twelve were given permits to solicit. That follow-up story was buried deep in the newspapers and never appeared on TV. There is no legal or legislative remedy for this because everyone has a First Amendment right to express his or her views, even when they are wrong. The solution is having strong voices to challenge this type of abuse of charities by politicians.

In conclusion, there are no silver bullets here. Giving exclusive power to the federal government or anyone else is far too dangerous. The best solution is permanent, continuous vigilance by charities and a strong willingness to stand up for their rights and cry "foul" when they see cases of abuse of charities, even if those charities are unpopular. The only overarching component of this is some type of national "Charity Defense Council" or "Charity Anti-Defamation League" that can educate, lobby, call out charity abuse, and, when necessary, litigate.

11. Repeal the Excess Holdings Rule, by Leslie Lenkowsky, Professor of Public Affairs and Philanthropic Studies, Indiana University, and Liaison, Bloomington Programs, Center on Philanthropy at Indiana University

Until the Bill and Melinda Gates Foundation came along, the wealthiest foundation in the world was in the Netherlands, the Stichtung Ingka Foundation. Created by Ingvar Kamprad, most of its assets were in a holding company that controlled IKEA, the home furnishings store he created.

Although this type of foundation is not unusual in Europe, American foundations, and the key people associated with them, usually cannot own more than a 20 percent interest in a particular business. This is because of a provision in the Tax Reform Act of 1969 known as the excess business holdings rule (section 4943 of the Internal Revenue Code). If they do, they face taxes and penalties that could surpass the value of their "excess" assets.

Section 4943 aimed at preventing donors from putting their companies in foundations to avoid paying taxes on their income while spending only a negligible amount on philanthropy. It also tried to prevent a large share of a corporation's stock from being held indefinitely by a single organization, thus protecting it from stock market pressures.

These concerns are not unreasonable. But the excess business holdings rule may not be the best way to deal with them.

If donors wanted to create a foundation chiefly to avoid paying taxes on their businesses, putting them in a foundation portfolio would not help. Though the donors might escape personal taxes, the companies would still owe applicable corporate taxes regardless of who or what owned them. Moreover, since 1969, private foundations have been required to use at least some of the income from their assets—currently 5 percent—for philanthropy. Donors are also not permitted to use these assets to benefit themselves or others associated with their foundations excessively.

Furthermore, foundation governing boards have to comply with a set of legal rules known as fiduciary duties. These rules oblige trustees to give priority to the interests of the charities for which they are responsible. For example, if a foundation might benefit financially from selling the shares of its donor's company, its trustees must have a compelling reason not to do so, or they might face penalties.

To be sure, enforcing these rules is often complicated and expensive. But the value of retaining the excess business holdings rule also has to be weighed against its costs. Section 4943 presents potential foundation donors with a choice: they can either create substantial grant-making organizations or stay active in their businesses, but they might not be able to do both unless their companies are a relatively small share of their assets. Moreover, by selling their businesses, donors might also be giving up money for grant making if other investments produced lower returns.

Ownership limits also restrict a foundation's ability to use its assets to achieve social purposes.* Section 4943 keeps grant makers from becoming large shareholders in companies that could generate jobs in an economically depressed area or whose operations cause problems such as pollution.

In other words, section 4943 makes less money available for philanthropy. It should be repealed.

12. Commit More Federal Funds for a Pay-for-Success Bond Program, by Marc J. Lane, President, Law Offices of Marc J. Lane, and Chair, Illinois Task Force on Social Innovation, Entrepreneurship, and Enterprise

Virtually hidden in President Obama's ill-fated 2012 budget was a $100 million allocation to test the efficacy of a "pay-for-success" bond initiative that just might help solve some of the nation's most vexing social problems. Pay-for-success is the American iteration of the social impact bond, an alternative model for financing social action introduced in Peterborough, England, in September 2010, and already the subject of broad support among enlightened policymakers around the world.

*I am grateful to my colleague, Richard Steinberg, for pointing this out.

The social impact bond is elegant in its simplicity. Not a bond in the traditional sense, where an investor is guaranteed a fixed return, the instrument is a contract among a government agency that agrees to pay for improved social outcomes, a private financing intermediary, and private investors.

The U.K. version was designed to fund innovative social programs that might reduce recidivism by ex-offenders and, with it, the public costs of housing and feeding repeat offenders. The problem was daunting: 60 percent of prisoners serving short-term sentences had historically gone on to reoffend within one year after release. The solution was to attract private investment to pay experienced social service organizations to provide intensive support to three thousand short-term prisoners, both before and after their release, in the hope that their preparation to reenter society would keep them out of the penal system.

The government decided which social goals would be supported, and how those goals would be achieved was left to the private sector. It was investors, through a bond-issuing organization, who ultimately endorsed the use of investment proceeds—how much would be invested in job training, drug rehabilitation, and other interventions.

If the plan shrinks recidivism rates by 7.5 percent or more, the government will repay the investors' capital and also share the taxpayers' savings with them, delivering up to a 13 percent return. If the plan doesn't succeed, the investment will have failed, and the government will owe the investors nothing.

The pay-for-success bond can create a futures contract in social outcomes at the very time that impact investors are demanding innovative solutions and measurable social results. It also shifts the risk of experimenting with promising but untested strategies from government to private capital markets, because public funds are expended only after targeted social benefits have actually been achieved.

But pay-for-success bonds are likely to prove s only if the proposed intervention is anticipated to g high enough net benefit to offer investors a reasonab return. The intervention must also have a measurable and credible outcome that positively correlates to a societal benefit.

The Departments of Justice and Labor are funding pay-for-success models to improve outcomes for past offenders and workers outside the economic mainstream. Other federal agencies should do no less.

13. Establish a New Taxonomy for Charities Focused on Meeting Needs and Achieving Outcomes, by Alexander Alvanos, Cofounder, Commonwealth Market

Charities work with great passion and dedication, often in difficult circumstances, striving to help individuals and families. It is incredibly important that they succeed in their work, but often they do not.

Let's consider the context that produces underperforming charities. These organizations are typically underresourced, their staff and leaders underpaid, and their directors spend much of their time desperately chasing grant dollars to fund programs. Answering the question, "How does our organization help?" is more important to funders than, "Why is our organization needed?" and "What does success look like?" Many programs aren't aligned with real needs and get lost along the way because no one has clearly defined success.

The misguided focus on programming starts at the inception of a charity. When applying for tax-exempt status from the IRS, an organization must choose a category from a range of classifications in the National Taxonomy of Exempt Entities (NTEE) based on what its programs do. But an "Adult and Child Matching Program" is meaningful only if a charity first understands the need of a specific youth population (for example, to develop conflict resolution skills) and then determines that an adult and child matching program can effectively meet this need. The NTEE's focus on activities promotes a culture of programming for the sake of programming that leads charities away from addressing people's needs.

When a charity observes increased youth violence in a community, understanding the root cause of the violence—say, lack of conflict resolution skills among young adults—is critical in developing an effective solution. Defining outcomes to meet the need, such as advancing social emotional learning to help build conflict-resolution skills, is then important to achieve success. Based on defined needs and outcomes, the charity can determine an appropriate program to achieve the desired results. Implementing an adult and child matching program does not have inherent value unless it is an appropriate program to meet a defined need. Understanding the need and intended outcomes of a target population is a reasonable requirement for any organization that aspires to serve people, apply for tax-exempt status, and ask others to commit their money and time.

The IRS must implement a new taxonomy based on what is needed for people to live healthy, productive, and meaningful lives. A new taxonomy should include need areas ranging from health to education and outcomes from providing preventative care to advancing social emotional learning. This encourages charities to think about "why" and "what" first, increasing the likelihood of achieving intended outcomes for the people they care about.

A new breed of charities is achieving unprecedented results for the people they serve. High-performing charities help the people they care about achieve the outcomes they deserve by continually measuring results and improving programs. The first step many high-performing charities take is understanding the needs of their target population and the outcomes that define their ultimate success. A needs-based classification would help more charities take this step on a path toward high performance and create better data so charities can develop meaningful collaborations focused on meeting needs.

14. Eliminate Stingy Benevolence, by Cassady V. Brewer, Assistant Professor, Georgia State University College of Law, Of Counsel, Morris, Manning & Martin, LLP*

Throughout my many years as an attorney advising high-net-worth clients, one thing has become increasingly clear: many wealthy individuals assuage their consciences by establishing charitable private foundations, but paradoxically they have no intention of ever truly giving up their wealth. Of course, there have been and are notable exceptions, yet a substantial majority of my wealthy clients demonstrated their philanthropy by funding a private foundation, appointing themselves and their children as decision makers, and then granting the minimum 5 percent per year to charities of their choice. The express goal of these pure grant-making foundations was perpetual existence by making minimum distributions without invading principal.

This is "stingy benevolence." It makes the donor feel good and has tax benefits, but it does little to move the philanthropic needle. Such stingy benevolence must change if we honestly and sincerely want a better world. I offer a simple proposal to accomplish this result.

Under U.S. income tax law, individuals generally may contribute to two basic types of charities and take a tax deduction

*The views expressed here are entirely those of the author and in no way represent the views of Georgia State University, the College of Law of Georgia State University, or Morris, Manning & Martin, LLP.

for their contributions. First, they may give up to 50 percent of their income to churches and so-called public (that is, well-established) charities. Essentially only the superwealthy give large, unrestricted gifts to public charities. The moderately wealthy, which I define as having $25 million to $100 million in assets, often choose another option: a private grant-making foundation.

A private foundation basically is a private charity. Individuals may contribute up to 30 percent of their income each year to these private charities during their lives and may contribute up to 100 percent of their wealth at their deaths. These wealthy donors (or their heirs) usually control these private charities and determine how much money to distribute each year from their private foundations to accomplish charitable purposes. The only significant constraint is that pursuant to the Internal Revenue Code, these private foundations must distribute at least 5 percent of the value of their assets each year or face a penalty tax.

Therefore, as long as a private foundation earns at least a 5 percent return, it never has to invade principal and can exist in perpetuity by distributing only 5 percent each year to charitable causes. Meanwhile, the wealthy donors (or their heirs) typically control the funds, pay themselves salaries, and attend foundation-paid conferences in pleasant locales, all the while extolling (over cocktails) the virtues of philanthropy.

The donor thus takes a tax deduction for the entire amount of the principal given away, but the principal never really leaves the donor's control. Only 5 percent per year is paid to charity, with the investment earnings on the principal generally covering that 5 percent minimum distribution. This makes no sense.

The solution is, in the case of pure grant-making foundations controlled by the donor or his or her family, to require that such foundations terminate after thirty years. Any money left in the foundation after thirty years becomes subject to a 100 percent tax payable to Uncle Sam. No exceptions. You snooze; you lose.

This is not a radical proposal. A forty-year term limit on private foundations was proposed in 1969 but eventually was dropped during floor debate in the Senate. Furthermore, the Bill and Melinda Gates Foundation, the largest in the world, promises to terminate within fifty years after Bill's and Melinda's deaths. Furthermore, the money the Gates Foundation will receive from Warren Buffett is scheduled to be spent within ten years after his estate has been settled. If the ultrarich can do this, why can't the moderately rich?

15. Create a More Open Giving Marketplace, by Art Taylor, President, Better Business Bureau Wise Giving Alliance

Many in the nonprofit sector have been pressing for better ways to get high-performing grant-seeking organizations together with institutional funders. Success would lead to greater access to funders, reduced fundraising costs, more innovative and diverse grant making, and greater mission impact.

We can increase the extent to which grant seekers focus and report on impact by getting funders to reward them for this work.

Charting Impact (CI), a new tool developed by the Better Business Bureau's Wise Giving Alliance, GuideStar, and Independent Sector, offers nonprofits a standard format to present information about the impact their work is having on society. Organizations can create concise, standardized reports about plans and progress that they ca[n] ... funders. It's far from perfect, but it has been ... substantial number of funders and grant seeker[s] ... value in it.

A reporting format is only a step on the road toward the goal of moving dollars to high-performing organizations. To accelerate progress, we should create grant-making gatherings that aggregate funders and grant seekers and put them together, literally, in a room. Funders that agree to participate and make a threshold amount of grants to the nonprofit organizations they interview in these gatherings would be entitled to certain tax benefits, to be defined.

The only way a grant seeker could get into the room would be to post a CI report and, based on that report, be invited by at least one funder. Meetings would be brief. CI reports require the grant seeker to make a concise case for funding and allow the funder to obtain vital information it would need in order to decide whether to go further.

Funders could meet only with organizations they have not funded within the past three years. This gathering would be for funders to learn about organizations new to them and for grant seekers to have direct access to institutions funding their line of work.

Funders would decide quickly if they intend to move forward with more traditional due diligence on a grant seeker and provide as much helpful feedback as possible. Grant seekers would also be asked to provide feedback to funders.

A one-day event of this type would potentially introduce a hundred funders to the leaders of between twenty-four and twenty-eight new prescreened grant seekers. This would go a long way toward making funders accessible to grant seekers that have felt shut out of institutional funding opportunities.

This concept could be repeated periodically and conducted regionally and locally. If it's successful, substantial funds could be shifted to higher-performing organizations.

16. The L3C: The For-Profit with the Nonprofit Soul, by Robert M. Lang, Founder, Americans for Community Development

I created L3C (Low-profit Limited Liability Company) as a business vehicle required to have a purpose without the cumbersome regulations embodied in the nonprofit sector. There are owners who can earn a fair living and share in profits. The L3C is all about doing good while making a reasonable return. I call it "the for-profit with the nonprofit soul." We have a long tradition in America of doing good while looking out for our financial self-interests. Some examples are old-fashioned barn raisings and the privateers who made up our Navy during the Revolution, who were in essence social entrepreneurs making a profit while doing the government's work.

The mill towns of the Industrial Revolution were a mix of charity and business. The mill owners built worker housing, buildings for businesses, churches, and so on. Our image of enterprising entrepreneurs of the nineteenth century usually does not conjure up a picture of a kindly grandfatherly type doing this strictly because he loved his workers. What he did understand was that happy workers usually worked harder, were less rowdy, and made his business more prosperous.

It does not take any imagination to see a thread of concepts we might call charitable intertwined with a goal of making money. Unfortunately, as we progressed through the twentieth century, we structured a society in which charity and making money are separate silos and never the twain should meet. Our current regulatory framework for nonprofits has institutionalized this concept to such an extent that nonprofits are forced to avoid financially beneficial situations.

What I recognized was that we needed a new way to perform charitable acts that could work within the regulatory environment that was now choking the nonprofit sector. The L3C is a for-profit structure created in the spirit of the natural arity and profit on which this country was built. It is ,t form of the LLC, which is a very flexible, well-thought- ,rmat for organizing businesses. It is perfect for entrepre- ırs who want the freedom of a partnership but the protection ı a corporation. An L3C is required by the state law under which it is organized to put charitable mission before profit.

A key to the successful capitalization of an L3C is turning the venture capital model on its head so the L3C has high-risk capital at a low cost. This can be provided by foundations using all or part of their required yearly 5 percent charitable distribution to invest in a for-profit for the purpose of furthering a charitable purpose. The L3C is the perfect entrepreneurial vehicle designed to further charitable purposes and support itself.

In the spirit of the National Civil Rights Act for Charity and Social Enterprise Act, Americans for Community Development has a bill before Congress, H.R. 3420, that will facilitate program-related investments. This bill will fundamentally change the charitable world, and the hope is that it will be the first step in unbridling charity from unneeded and oppressive regulation.

17. Pay for Performance in the Charitable Sector: Private Foundations, by Lawrence Mendenhall, Vice President, General Counsel, and Secretary, Humanity United

What should *pay for performance* mean in the charitable sector? For operating nonprofits that raise money to provide direct services to specific communities, measures of impact (for example, clients served or funds raised) can potentially be translated into performance and compensation benchmarks for management.

The task is more difficult for grant-making private foundations. Foundations are typically endowed by their founders, so there's no need for fundraising. They also tend to lack direct operations, so judging their direct impact on specific communities is more difficult. The only legally mandated measure of success for a private foundation is whether the foundation has spent 5 percent of the value of its net investment assets on charitable purposes in any given year, without regard to effectiveness. Put another way, although a foundation must spend, there is no minimum amount of "good" that a foundation's giving must buy.

In an attempt to show impact, many foundations establish internal goals and objectives to gauge their success, creating elaborate, foundation-specific taxonomies to track the impact of their efforts. Some foundations go further, incorporating institutional goals into their performance management systems. Managers are encouraged to take risks in their grant making to achieve these goals.

In reality, however, failure to meet these self-imposed goals rarely causes the compensation of foundation managers to drop. Compensation is set, instead, by benchmarking managers' salaries, not their performance, against the salaries of managers at other foundations, known as "comparables" or "comps." The process is often very outcome driven, with the results ensuring that the foundation's managers receive precisely the compensation they decide to award themselves. Left out is the fact that the risk of failure rests almost entirely outside the private foundation. What exactly is the risk? It is that the foundation's grant funds will be wasted on efforts that do not achieve their stated goals, leaving the money unavailable for other charitable work. In this way, the communities and organizations that rely on the foundation's funding bear the risks of the decisions of foundation managers, not the managers themselves.

What is the answer? A modest start would be to ask foundations to share publicly their goals, as well as whether and how these are used to judge foundation manager performance. The federal tax form that foundations file annually, the Form

990-PF, could be amended to include these questions. This would encourage foundations to make their internal goals public and use those goals to judge manager performance. Private foundations would also benefit from seeing each other's taxonomies, potentially leading to shared measures of performance that could someday serve as true comparables in the compensation-setting process.

The IRS has pioneered this approach on the tax form that public charities file, prompting charities to adopt conflict-of-interest policies, share their internal governance documents, and publicize their financial statements simply by asking questions about these topics (for example, "Does the organization have a written conflict of interest policy?"). Questions for foundations might include, "Does the organization prepare written internal goals to measure its progress?" "Does it make these goals available publicly?" and "Does it incorporate the accomplishments of these goals into performance benchmarks for managers?"

Pay for performance in the charitable sector will always be imperfect, especially in the foundation context. However, asking a few simple questions on the Form 990-PF would encourage private foundations to bring their goal setting to light and use progress toward their goals to judge the performance of foundation managers. Adopting this approach would help bring private foundations one step closer to true pay for performance.

Where We Go from Here

It was not my intention for this chapter to propose the basis for a national legislative act. I wanted to, first, show the huge policy opportunities we are not taking advantage of; second, argue that we deserve a sweeping national legislative vision; and third, start the conversation about what such a vision might look like. And the good news is that when asked to consider it, leaders in the field have innovative, intelligent ideas about policy changes that reflect the situation we find ourselves in today.

The next step is to launch the conversation formally. The Charity Defense Council will undertake the effort, which must collect thoughtful opinion and counsel on the subject from all corners.

At the same time, this effort cannot and should not try to be all things to all people. It will have a strong point of view: that it is time to liberate the humanitarian sector from the economic constraints that hold it back. It will stand on a set of clear principles related to that point of view. It will not waver on those principles or betray them. If those who wish to further encumber the sector with regulation and constraint seek legislative efforts to do so, they will have to do it elsewhere.

This is the first step: to get the conversation started and create a formal clearinghouse for ideas and draw them out. This is no small task. Pulling ideas out of unconsciousness, or discovering them in places where we don't even know they exist, requires as much effort as raising money or getting votes. It will require a strong organizing effort with strong follow-through.

We should begin this task immediately, and our goal should be to achieve a final draft by 2015. We will use the full force of the community drawn to the Charity Defense Council to achieve this.

6

Organize Ourselves

Come together, right now.
JOHN LENNON

If you are alcoholic, you can find a twelve-step program in any city, held at any time of day, to connect with others for help. If you own a Smart Car, you can go to meetup.org and find other Smart Car owners in your area who are organizing a Sunday Smart Car drive. If you are a gay hockey player, you can go to gayhockey.org and find out about local teams and tournaments. If you like to knit, there are knitting shops, knitting guilds, knitting classes, knitting group ratings on Yelp, and more.

But if you believe that we need to change the way the public thinks about charity and give the humanitarian sector the same economic freedoms we give to the rest of the economy and if you want to make this your cause, where do you go to get involved? What can you do? Who can you call?

Until today, the answer has been, "Nowhere, nothing, and no one."

But today, that changes. As of today there are places you can go to get involved, things you can do, a community with which you can connect, and a Web site you can go to. And there will be a lot more of all this as people discover real and meaningful ways to get engaged.

Here are seventeen actions you can take now to help get this effort going.

1 Become a Member

The Charity Defense Council will be funded with contributions from institutions and individuals alike. You can go to charitydefensecouncil.org right now and register.

2 Donate

Make the transformation of causes your new lifelong cause. Consider what you can do to support it beyond becoming a member. You can make a major gift to the Charity Defense Council at several levels, all of which can be paid over time.

3 Start a Local "Nonprofits Anonymous" Discussion Group

The success of the Charity Defense Council as an organization will be determined by the strength of the bonds we create with one another. Virtual community has its place, but it pales in comparison to the strength of real community. There is no substitute for human contact. If we build community face-to-face, we will be stronger for it. And it will increase the power of everything we do online because we will know one another beyond our usernames.

I can tell you after speaking at more than a hundred and twenty conferences in the past three years, and participating in dozens of panels and workshops, that people in this sector have valuable ideas and experiences and a contagious passion to contribute. None of this potential can be fully harnessed online.

But even face-to-face community building is only as powerful as the effort and the energy we put into it. We want to create a great network of local meetings, not dissimilar to what Bill W. created with the twelve-step program of Alcoholics Anonymous. That began in 1955. Today, in the United States alone, AA has over 1.2 million members in some fifty-seven thousand groups.[1] These people meet to discuss their difficulties and share their strength and hope. We can adopt this model and create local groups that meet once a month to discuss common problems and share solutions. We can stay abreast of the progress that our local, regional, and national efforts are achieving.

The meetings will have another powerful purpose. We can form book and blog discussion groups to advance cutting-edge ideas. I am consistently amazed by the innovative thinking published by thought leaders in our sector every single day. I learn something new and important every time I read them. Imagine if there were tens of thousands of us all engaging with innovative ideas all the time. Imagine what new thinking and fruitful collaboration would come of it.

You can go to the Charity Defense Council Web site and sign up to chair one of these groups. Find people in your town or city who work in the sector and care about these issues. This will create vibrant groups that represent a cross-section of the community. By using residential geography as a common denominator, you won't get siloed with the other people working on your issue. You'll meet people working on breast cancer, the environment, at-risk youth, epilepsy, suicide prevention, and all of the other important issues. People will begin to see the common challenges we face and identify common solutions and, more important, common passion. Each group will be part of a larger regional network, which will be part of a national network. What a force we can be!

Organizing by residential geography will also make it convenient to meet. On our Web site you'll see suggestions for discussion topics, local guest speakers, meeting format, governance, guidelines, and rules of order. That will put us all on the same operating system in real time. If you want to go to a meeting in another area, you'll be acclimated before you even walk in. And like the 12-step program, we'll have intergroup meetings at which the chairs of local meetings can meet and share what works.

4 Hold an Introductory Office Meeting at Your Organization's Offices, and Commit to Bringing in at Least Five New Members

Schedule a sixty-minute introductory meeting at which your coworkers can learn about the Council and have the opportunity to register. The Council's Web site provides a suggested meeting format, logistical instructions, registration materials, and a supporting video that you can screen at the meeting.

Hosting one of these introductions serves the dual purpose of building membership for the council and the cause and advancing the culture of your own organization. Over the past three years, I've been able to observe how much our own organizational cultures reinforce the economic constraints that keep us from fulfilling our own potential. Imagine if everyone at your organization were a member of the Charity Defense Council. Imagine everyone aligned on a set of values that creates a new context for your work.

5 Sign On to Our Rapid Response Media Team

When the next sensational, one-sided media story comes out on one of our own organizations, we want to deliver a powerful response. To do that, we need a large, committed group of people to write letters, post comments, and make phone calls in response. With that force in place, we can demand and secure retractions, if appropriate, and get equal time for alternative points of view. We can get meetings with editors and investigative staff. We can inundate news Web site comment sections with alternative points of view. We can use our national reach to organize national and local protests of the media outlets, and those demonstrations can become media stories in and of themselves, bringing valuable publicity to our cause at low cost. We can become a voting bloc that offers annual awards to the media outlets that have demonstrated the best practices in reporting on the sector.

We've never had such a tool at our disposal. It's impossible to imagine all of the ways that it could actually move our cause forward.

6 Sign On to Our Rapid Response Public Policy Team

We have to organize to prevent and respond to bad public policy, so that when the next piece of bad policy is proposed, we can deliver a powerful response. With the exception of a few cases, we have never done that before. With this team in place, we can fill the in-boxes of the elected officials and regulators who make these proposals with our own thoughtful, reasoned arguments in opposition. We want to impress these officials with the depth of our knowledge about the unintended consequences of their proposals. This is another reason that it's so important for us to get involved in reading circles and face-to-face meetings with our peers: so we can be real experts in our own field. Public officials aren't going to respond to us only because of our numbers. We have to communicate about a better way.

We will coordinate these campaigns with the actions of our legal team. If our initial engagements don't lead to reconsideration of the proposed measures, we can use our numbers and our arguments to undertake civil actions—physical demonstrations that send a more powerful signal and engage the media.

7 Sign On to Our One-Thing-a-Day List

There's something each of us can be doing every day. It won't take much time—five minutes a day—but it can have a significant cumulative effect and can keep us all engaged in the transformation we are committed to.

Every day we'll send you a request for action. On Monday you might write a personal e-mail to a friend in the sector to ask if he will become a member of the council. On Tuesday you ask your dentist if she'll put a display box of "I'm overhead" flyers in her waiting room. On Wednesday you might call your hometown newspaper to ask if it will do a story on the work of the Charity Defense Council. On Thursday you distribute five "I'm overhead" buttons to co-workers. On Friday you send an e-mail to the governor of Utah, for example, as part of a national effort to get Utah to repeal an onerous piece of regulation targeting the humanitarian sector.

You might be thinking that this sounds like a bit of a pain. But consider the sea change we are trying to achieve and the impact of thousands of people like you doing thousands of things like this day after day. Consider what it will feel like to be a part of something this big.

8 Submit Stories for Our Research Project on the Negative Effects of Lack of Investment in Overhead

In 2006 the Nonprofit Overhead Cost Project at Indiana University studied the impact of suppressed spending on overhead and found that the organizations that spent more on their own organizational strength and capacity had superior programs. This ran completely counter to the conventional wisdom that the best organizations are the ones that send the highest percentage of donor dollars to the cause, as traditionally defined. While the project looked at a massive number of Form 990s to get certain reporting data, they were able to conduct only nine site surveys. We want to add substantially to the body of data on this subject, both for our own purposes and to advance the academic literature.

You can help by volunteering your organization for study and submitting your own experience on the subject for study. We are looking to identify the opportunity costs of inadequate spending on organizational capacity. So if you have experienced or witnessed a situation in which a shortsighted emphasis on current spending caused detrimental effects on programs, we want to hear from you.

As an example, the Nonprofit Overhead Cost Project pointed to a suicide hotline that had inadequate investment in technology, which resulted in distressed callers receiving a busy signal when they called in.

9 Help Us Recruit Great "I'm Overhead" Stories

We want to create a large and ongoing archive of testimonials from those who are categorized in budgets as "overhead." The archive will give us a rich trove of candidates from which to select subjects for our ads. In addition, the sheer quantity of subjects will convey another story, this one about the army of unsung heroes out there who support the causes we all love while being stigmatized as a burden. We will integrate this archive into our Web site and, in our ads, direct consumers to that section of the site. The ad will be the first step in their education. It will show them a beautiful and compelling group of people, all categorized as not-part-of-the-cause but all fiercely dedicated to their cause. Members can also use the archive to make new connections and create new networks of like-minded colleagues.

10 Organize Regional Seminars for Board Members

People often come to me after a speech and say they wish that their board members had been there—they're the ones who really need to hear this message because they hold the reins.

Those audience members often ask me, "What c… my board members that will change their thinking about o… head, advertising, risk taking, and so on?" In fact, there are no silver bullet words that will turn a board member around in five minutes. Instead we should be asking, "What ongoing process can I engage my board members in to transform their thinking?"

Board members are a huge lever when it comes to achieving economic freedom. But the ultimate lever is still the cultural mind-set at large: the general public. Even the most enlightened and sympathetic board member will feel compelled to respond to what the public wants. No one wants to be the board member on whose watch the charity's watchdog rating fell by two stars—even if the board member doesn't believe in the validity of the rating.

Nonetheless, it's hard to underestimate the impact that a transformation in a board's thinking can have. We want to make an array of effective tools available to humanitarian sector leaders so that they can start creating that transformation. We want to make an entire curriculum available, complete with speakers and local experts.

We will put large groups of board members together on a regional basis. The whole enterprise will be more powerful if participants work as a group rather than remaining siloed by organization. And members from any one organization are likely to get onboard faster and more enthusiastically if they see that they're not sticking their necks out on their own but that many other organizations are out there too. Also, when gathered together with their board members, organizations can commit to powerful collective actions that they couldn't commit to or envision locked in a room on their own. And it's a lot more efficient to organize one curriculum for a couple of dozen organizations than it is to organize one for each of them.

We are looking for powerful local leaders who have the influence to organize such training programs in their city.

In this capacity, you could literally transform the culture of charity in your area.

11 Organize Regional Seminars for Major Donors

Many of the same arguments apply to major donors who are not board members. We are looking for people who will take on the task of coordinating tandem programs specifically designed for major donors at the local level. These donors are not only key to organizational strategy because of their influence, but they are also potential donors for the structural transformation work that the Charity Defense Council will undertake.

12 Sponsor an All-Staff Presentation at Your Organization

Until someone paints the whole picture for them, people don't fully appreciate how confining the box is in which they've been asked to work. Once they see that picture, the transformation is swift and apparent. The fire that got them interested in this work in the first place is suddenly rekindled because they now have a full understanding of why they haven't been able to create change. As much as we have to enlighten the general public, board members, and major donors, we have to enlighten ourselves and our colleagues and peers.

Call and tell us that you'll organize an all-staff orientation at your own organization.

13 Ask Your State Legislator to Come to a Regional Meeting, and Get Her to Say Yes

State legislators are another fundamental lever, but they won't take hours out of their day to learn more about how the humanitarian sector works unless they think 70 percent of the rest of the legislature is going to be there. We need people who will take on the task of getting their state senators and state representatives to attend a regional conference of legislators to address the Charity Defense Council's core issues. You won't be working alone; dozens of other people in your area will have made the same commitment to get their legislators to attend.

14 Work with Local Media to Get Ad Space Donated

Can you get your local newspaper to run a full-page version of our "I'm overhead" ad for no charge? Will you work on getting your local radio and television stations to become sponsors of the campaign for the year? We won't be satisfied with donated advertising substituting for the paid advertising that the big guns of consumer brand advertising use, but we won't turn down donated space. Every message that's out there is better than one that isn't. We need local people like you on the ground, persistently cultivating relationships with local media to help us get these placements.

15 Reach Out to Five Charities and Ask If They've Heard About This Effort

This is simple: send a thoughtful, enthusiastic e-mail or letter to five peers at other organizations asking if they've heard about the Charity Defense Council and explaining your own enthusiasm about the effort.

16 Wear the "I'm Overhead" Shirt, Post the Bumper Sticker, Put up the Poster at Your Office, Fly the Flag in Your Reception Area, and Share the Ideas in This Book with Others

Like any other cause, we literally need to wear our hearts on our sleeves. So our Web site has an array of powerful merchandise to help you help us distinguish this as a new cause. You can choose from a selection of T-shirts, get a Charity Defense Council flag to fly in your reception area, and find posters, bumper stickers, and other educational items. Imagine how hard it will be for your executive team to say they have to worry about overhead when there's a fleet of "I'm overhead" shirts at the next budget meeting. Imagine walking down the street and having someone ask you what "I'm overhead" means. You get to start the conversation on your terms instead of being on the defensive.

17 Be Creative; We Haven't Thought of Everything Here

You might have an idea for an ad, a funding source, a funder we should approach, an idea about legislation, or something else.

Send it to the Charity Defense Council. We not only want your ideas, we want you to think of more. It could very well be that the key to our success has not been identified yet.

As I said at the outset, the question people ask me the most after each talk I give is, "What can I do?" This chapter offers some answers. There are many meaningful things you can do right now to help steer the course of change, starting today.

7

You Cannot Stop the Spring

Nothing is as powerful as an idea whose time has come.
VICTOR HUGO

It's been forty-two years since I was eight years old and watched Neil Armstrong walk on the moon. And yet in my mind, it remains the last great thing that this nation achieved. I believe we achieved it because we set a goal to achieve it, and that in the absence of that goal, we'd still be trying to figure it out how to get there. There is evidence for this hypothesis. We landed on the moon on July 20, 1969—precisely eight years and fifty-six days from the time President Kennedy set the goal on May 25, 1961, before a joint session of Congress. And yet as recently as 2004, the Bush administration said that it would take us at least twice as long—sixteen years—to return to the moon.[1] The Obama administration has scrapped plans for it altogether.

Deadlines Make All the Difference

How is it possible that in 1969, in an age when we had never before gone to the moon, didn't know how to, and didn't have a computer more powerful than a calculator, we got there in eight years? Yet in an age when we already have a complete set of blueprints for doing it, have done it, have people around who were there when we did it and who know how to do it, and have unspeakably powerful computing power, we believe it will take us twice as long to get there again?

The reason is simple: what we say we will do changes what we believe we can do. And right now, we are unwilling to commit ourselves to getting back to the moon—to say that we will—by any specific date. In the absence of a vision, human destiny is left to the experts, and experts lack vision.

Deadlines make the difference. They transform the conversation. They alter context. They light human beings up. They make a mockery of all previous expertise about the limits of human potential.

Werner Erhard deconstructed all of this when he launched the Hunger Project. He unearthed the notion that a powerful context changes everything. You give rise to a radical new conversation when you say, as John Kennedy did, "I believe that this nation should commit itself to achieving the goal, before this decade is out, of landing a man on the moon and returning him safely to the Earth."[2]

Once you set the goal, people begin to tell you it cannot be done. That is already something new. Then they start to tell you why it cannot be done. Then you're really getting somewhere, because until then, you never knew why it couldn't be done, and until you know why it cannot be done, you cannot possibly do it. For example, someone says you cannot get to the moon because it requires a landing vehicle. A landing vehicle is heavy. In order to get a landing vehicle to escape velocity, you need a powerful booster rocket. So you start to work on the booster rocket. Et voilà, you're on your way to the moon. A fundamental problem that has to be solved in order to get to the moon is being discussed. Prior to the setting of a deadline, it was not.

There was no reason to. And there was certainly no urgency to discuss it. The deadline was the catalyst for breakthrough at a greatly accelerated pace.

That's why we can get to the moon faster in 1969 than in 2012.

I believe that our sector needs more daring goals. Rather than saying, "Let's try to get this done faster," we have to hold ourselves to fixed dates by which things will happen.

I applaud Share Our Strength, which has set a five-year deadline for the end of child hunger in America. I applaud the National Breast Cancer Coalition (a client of my firm) for setting a nine-year deadline for the end of breast cancer.

The Charity Defense Council can set no less ambitious a standard for its own work. Therefore, I believe that we must commit ourselves to reversing public opinion polls about charity within the next ten years. In other words, where just 10 percent of Americans now think that charities do a "very good job" spending money wisely, in ten years, that percentage will be reversed: 90 percent of Americans will think that.[3] And where 70 percent of Americans now believe that charities waste a great deal or a fair amount of money, in ten years, 70 percent of people *won't* believe that.

The bigger goal, which reversing public opinion will support, must be to increase charitable giving from the current 2 to 3 percent of gross domestic product within ten years, an additional $150 billion of giving. And if we can have it go disproportionately to health and human services causes, which now receive perhaps $60 billion worth of annual contribution revenue, we can, in ten years, more than double the amount of money going to those causes. That's a goal worth fighting for. That's changing the world.

Let's Think Huge

I believe we can achieve these ambitious goals because there are massive areas of opportunity that we are not exploiting. If we were already doing everything we possibly could to make these goals a reality, I wouldn't be optimistic. But it can almost be said that we are doing none of the things that we possibly could. Once we start taking advantage of the vast landscapes of opportunities I have tried to describe in this book, and each action begins interacting with each other action, transformative things will begin to happen—things we never previously thought could happen.

Consider the potential that exists in any one of the areas to which we will commit ourselves.

First, we will bring our case to the public and the media with a serious anti-defamation strategy and the apparatus to carry it out. This has never been done before. To lament that we cannot change the media environment in which we operate is like a defense lawyer lamenting that the jury is sure to convict his client because he doesn't plan to offer any defense.

Second, we will begin to make our case to the public by engaging in a thoughtful, provocative, and ongoing conversation with the public using paid media. This has never been done before. Until we've challenged the assumption, we can't lament that public opinion is fixed, immovable, or set in stone.

Third, we will make our case in the courts and to the regulatory apparatus at a scale not yet achieved. And this defense will reverberate in the media and the public discourse.

Fourth, we will carry our case to Capitol Hill with a compelling legislative agenda—one that has not only never been previously brought but never been contemplated. This too will create a conversation in the media and in the public. It will elevate our issues to new heights among elected officials and the electorate because, for the first time, we will make the discussion and consideration of our issues a priority.

And fifth, we will create a massive movement—an organization of our own ranks, with purpose, direction, and assignments. When the breast cancer community organized itself, the National Breast Cancer Coalition, the Revlon Walk, the Race for the Cure, the Breast Cancer 3-Days, and a hundred other initiatives resulted. Those things exist because people rallied under the banner of their cause to fight for a transformation in their conditions. Imagine if the AIDS community had never organized itself, the gay and lesbian community had never organized itself, the African American community had never organized itself. We in the humanitarian sector have never organized ourselves for our own cause because it never occurred to us that our own liberation *is* a cause unto itself.

So it is a wide open frontier out there—all possibility and potential.

Now consider the size of the potential represented by combining those five separate areas of opportunity. Think about what happens when they all intersect in one integrated and coordinated effort. Imagine a large paid advertising campaign that's coordinated at the local, regional, and national levels with a powerful grassroots organizing effort that's synchronized with discussions with reporters. Think about a challenge to an unconstitutional local fundraising regulation that's coordinated with our national grassroots network that's integrated with outreach to investigative reporters that's linked to new legislative proposals to prevent these kinds of obstructions in the future. Think about a reporter considering a sensational story on a large national charity being inundated with e-mails from our grassroots network, directed to an array of user-friendly information tools on the Web, contacted by state officials who are now advocating on our behalf because of our legal defense operations, and contacted by a few other reporters who met us at a national convention for investigative reporters and who have been moved to support our side.

We despair about the future when we believe that no real change is possible. Sean Penn was asked by a reporter during the Los Angeles riots in the 1990s why he thought poor people were looting and torching their own neighborhoods instead of invading Beverly Hills. He responded that if they went into Beverly Hills, that would mean they had some hope that things could actually change, but they didn't—they were completely without hope—so they destroyed their own.

The conditions under which the humanitarian sector does its work no longer need to seem hopeless, fixed, or inevitable. We no longer have to believe that this is the way it is and the way it always will be. There is a way forward.

We can dare to be excited and inspired. We can give ourselves permission to dream, be impassioned, and have fun because the future we have been resigned to isn't going to occur. A different future—a purposeful, unfathomably productive, impossible future—is going to occur. It's a future we get to create.

The poet Pablo Neruda said that you can pick all of the flowers, but you cannot stop the spring. Transforming the way the general public thinks about charity is an idea whose time has come, and we are the lucky ones who find ourselves alive during its moment. This transformation is charity's destiny, and the making of it is ours.

All we have to do is not say no to it.

Notes

Special Note

1. I first heard this description used by Allen Grossman, a professor at Harvard Business School.

Chapter One

1. J. Altucher, "How to Become a Superhero (or . . . Why I Would Never Donate to a Major Charity)," *Freakonomics*, Mar. 29, 2011, http://www.freakonomics.com/2011/03/29/how-to-become-a-superhero-or...why-i-would-never-donate-to-a-major-charity/.
2. J. Wang, "Don't Donate Money to Charity," *Bargaineering*, Feb. 24, 2009, http://www.bargaineering.com/articles/dont-donate-money-to-charity.html.
3. A. de Tocqueville, *Democracy in America: Part the Second, The Social Influence of Democracy*, trans. Henry Reeve (New York: J. & H. G. Langley, 1840), p. 11.
4. R. H. Bremner, *American Philanthropy*, 2nd ed. (Chicago: University of Chicago Press, 1988), p. 42.
5. D. M. Pallotta, *Uncharitable* (Medford, Mass.: Tufts University Press, 2008), p. 130.
6. Bremner, p. 190.
7. Ibid.
8. P. C. Light, "Rebuilding Trust in Charity," Brookings Institution, May 16, 2012, http://www.brookings.edu/opinions/2002/0516nonprofits_light.aspx.

9. B. Gose, "42% of Americans Say Relief Effort Damaged Faith in Nonprofit Groups," *Chronicle of Philanthropy*, Sept. 5, 2002, http://philanthropy.com/article/42-of-Americans-Say-Relief/51500/.
10. Ellison Research, "Americans' Perceptions of the Financial Efficiency of Non-Profit Organizations," Feb. 2008, http://www.ellisonresearch.com/releases/0208_ERWhitePaper.pd.
11. P. C. Light, "How Americans View Charities: A Report on Charitable Confidence, 2008," Brookings Institution, Apr. 2008, http://www.brookings.edu/papers/2008/04_nonprofits_light.asp.
12. Ibid.
13. Ibid.
14. F. Newport, "Congress' Job Approval Entrenched at Record Low of 13%," *Gallup Politics*, Nov. 14, 2011, http://www.gallup.com/poll/150728/congress-job-approval-entrenched-record-low.aspx.
15. R. F. Kennedy, speech given at the University of Pennsylvania, May 6, 1964, http://www.thisdayinquotes.com/2011/05/about-one-fifth-of-people-are-against.html.
16. P. Miller and T. H. Johnson, *The Puritans: A Sourcebook of Their Writings, Two Volumes Bound as One* (Mineola, N.Y.: Dover, 2001), p. 195.
17. ONE, "About," http://www.one.org/c/us/about/3782/, accessed Feb. 2012.
18. R. W. Emerson, "Nature," in *Emerson's Prose and Poetry*, ed. Joel Porte and Saundra Morris (New York: Norton, 2001), p. 27.
19. Pallotta TeamWorks, "Record of Impact: Detailed Financial Disclosure," http://www.pallottateamworks.com/financial_detailed.php, accessed Feb. 2012.
20. Ibid.
21. Ibid.
22. M. D. Young, "Partial Final Award and Statement of Reasons," *Pallotta TeamWorks* v. *Avon Products Foundation, Inc.*, no. 1420011424. Judicial Arbitration and Mediation Services, New York, July 15, 2005.
23. The $70.9 million figure for the 2002 Pallotta TeamWorks event is based on gross participant income of $145,372,218 (from the Avon 2002 financial statements) and subtracts $2 million in proceeds from Kiss Goodbye to Breast Cancer, according to an Avon press release ("Avon Foundation Continues Commitment to Breast Cancer Cause[/]Awards Nearly $30

Million in Grants to Thirteen Organizations," CDC Foundation press release, Sept. 24, 2002, accessed Mar. 30, 2012, http://www.cdcfoundation.org/pr/2002/avon-foundation-continues-commitment-breast-cancer-cause) for an adjusted gross participant income of $143,372,218. The net figure specified for Pallotta TeamWorks is calculated by subtracting from the adjusted gross participant income the sum of (1) event expenses of $71,852,150 shown as fundraising (from Avon 2002 financial statements) and (2) $596,000 in estimated expenses from Avon's Kiss Goodbye to Breast Cancer event, using a $2 million income figure ("Avon Foundation Continues Commitment to Breast Cancer Cause") and applying its 30 percent cost ratio from the 2001 Kiss Goodbye event. The figure does not include income or expenses for Avon's 2002 Boogie for Breast Cancer event. The gross figure for Avon for 2003 is based on $26,928,695 in "special events income" plus a $3,600,656 contribution from Avon Products less $2 million for Kiss Goodbye to Breast Cancer, which PR Newswire said "is expected to raise $2 million." The net figure for the Avon 2003 event is calculated by subtracting from the gross income the sum of (1) $10,231,852 in total event expenses shown as fundraising (from the Avon 2003 financial statements) and (2) $7,822,416 in joint costs allocated to the Breast Cancer Crusade (also from Avon 2003 financial statements), and adding back $596,000 in already deducted estimated expenses from the Kiss Goodbye to Breast Cancer event (using a $2 million income figure from "Avon Foundation Honors 'The Most Powerful Women in Breast Cancer' at Annual Kiss Goodbye to Breast Cancer Awards Celebration," Avon press release, Oct. 14, 2003) and applying its 30 percent cost ratio from the 2001 Kiss Goodbye event. Joint costs are deducted in order to achieve a fair comparison, as no event-related costs were allocated to programs on the 2002 Pallotta TeamWorks figures.

24. D. Tinkelman, "Breast Cancer Walks: Linking Organizational Stresses and Questionable Accounting Practices," working paper presented at ARNOVA conference, Philadelphia, Nov. 2007, p. 19.
25. G. Overholser and S. Stannard-Stockton, "Philanthropic Equity," *Tactical Philanthropy* (blog), Jan. 21, 2009, http://www.tacticalphilanthropy.com/2009/01/philanthropic-equity.
26. U.S. Department of the Treasury, Internal Revenue Service, "Exempt Organizations Business Master File," Sept. 2011, from The Urban Institute,

National Center for Charitable Statistics, http://nccsdataweb.urban.org, accessed Sept. 2011.

27. M. R. Kramer, "Catalytic Philanthropy," *Stanford Social Innovation Review*, Fall 2009, pp. 30–35, http://www.ssireview.org/images/ads/2009FA_feature_Kramer.pd.
28. L. Simone, e-mail message to author, Aug. 26, 2010.
29. A. Geiss, e-mail message to author, Apr. 30, 2010.
30. C. H. Wadhwani, e-mail message to author, Sept. 29, 2009.
31. R. Kao, e-mail message to author, June 28, 2009.
32. L. Villalon, e-mail message to author, Apr. 23, 2010.
33. P. Murray, e-mail message to author, Apr. 30, 2010.
34. J. Hancock, e-mail message to author, May 4, 2010.
35. D. Doering, e-mail message to author, Feb. 16, 2011.
36. P. Maehara, e-mail message to author.
37. B. Osborn, e-mail message to author, Mar. 13, 2007.

Chapter Two

1. "CNN Clip of Grassley interview About Boys and Girls Club," Cable New Network, Mar. 12, 2010, video clip, http://www.youtube.com/watch?v=hmUZLu7VvP4, accessed Feb. 2012.
2. Ibid.
3. B. Zlatos, "Boys & Girls Clubs Outlook Clouded by National Dispute," *Pittsburgh Tribune-Review*, Mar. 30, 2010, http://www.pittsburghlive.com/x/pittsburghtrib/news/s_674014.html. M. Jaffe, "Boys & Girls' Club CEO Roxanne Spillett's $1M Total Compensation Under Fire," *ABC News*, Mar. 12, 2010, http://abcnews.go.com/Business/boys-girls-club-ceo-roxanne-spilletts-1m-salary/story?id=10086264#.TyyGSZgVcfM.
4. Zlatos.
5. "Boys & Girls Clubs of America Names New President and CEO," Boys & Girls Club of America press release, June 16, 2011, http://www.bgca.org/newsevents/PressReleases/Pages/NewPresCEO_061611.aspx.
6. S. Perry, "Senators Call On Boys & Girls Clubs of America to Justify Pay and Spending," *Chronicle of Philanthropy*, Mar. 12, 2010, http://philanthropy.com/article/Senators-Call-On-Boys-Girls/64665/.
7. Jaffe.

8. Ibid.
9. R. Nakashima, "Disney CEO Received $51.1M in Compensation in 2008," *Breitbart*, Jan. 16, 2009, http://www.breitbart.com/article.php?id =D95OJM081&show_article=1.
10. Forbes, "Profile: Steve Ballmer," Sept. 2011, http://www.forbes.com/ profile/steve-ballmer/.
11. E. Fredrix, "PepsiCo CEO Gets $14.9M in '08, Up from '07," *Boston.com*, Mar. 25, 2009, http://www.boston.com/business/articles/2009 /03/25/pepsico_ceo_gets_149m_in_08_up_from_07/.
12. Hibbard, James, "Top TV Salaries: Winfrey, Seacrest, Sheen, Laurie," Reuters, U.S. edition, Aug. 11, 2010, http://www.reuters.com/article/2010 /08/11US-television-salariesidUSTRE67A50x20100811.
13. Lockheed Martin, *2009 Annual Report*, http://www.lockheedmartin.com /content/dam/lockheed/data/corporate/documents/2009-Annual-report .pdf, accessed Apr. 2012.
14. Forbes, "CEO Compensation: #64 Robert J. Stevens," Apr. 28, 2010, http:// www.forbes.com/lists/2010/12/boss-10_Robert-J-Stevens_RIMI.html.
15. "CNN Clip of Grassley Interview About Boys and Girls Club."
16. Jaffe.
17. I. Wilhem, "Charity Expert Defends Boys & Girls Clubs in Pay Controversy," *Chronicle of Philanthropy*, Mar. 16, 2010, http://philanthropy.com /blogs/giveandtake/charity-expert-defends-boys-girls-clubs-in-pay -controversy/21849.
18. Perry.
19. Ibid.
20. Jaffe.
21. S. Ohlemacher, "Charity CEO Pay Questioned: Senators Want Answers over Nonprofit Leader's $1 Million Compensation," *Huffington Post*, Mar. 12, 2010, http://www.huffingtonpost.com/2010/03/12/charity-ceo -pay-questione_n_496317.html.
22. Zlatos.
23. S. Ohlemacher, "Senators Question $1 Million Pay for Charity's CEO," *Seattle Times*, http://seattletimes.nwsource.com/html/businesstechnology /2011324615_apuscharityexpenses.html, accessed Mar. 30, 2012.
24. Conversation with author, Aug. 22, 2011.

25. N. Lewis, "Spillett to Retire as BGCA President, Clark Named Successor," *Youth Today*, June 17, 2011, http://www.youthtoday.org/view_article.cfm?article_id=4850.
26. D. E. Blum, "Nonprofit Leadership Still Shaky, Study Finds," *Chronicle of Philanthropy*, June 26, 2011, http://philanthropy.com/article/Two-Thirds-of-Nonprofit/128007/.
27. "CNN Clip of Grassley Interview About Boys and Girls Club."
28. Associated Press, "Lobbying Expenses Hit Record High in 2009," *CBS News*, Feb. 12, 2010, http://www.cbsnews.com/stories/2010/02/12/politics/main6202526.shtml.
29. K. Crowley, "Head of AIDS Charity Complaining About Loss of Public Funding Rakes in $363K a Year," *New York Post*, Apr. 25, 2011, http://www.nypost.com/p/news/local/living_high_on_aids_BMvRiaZypXnyEnq7nUAomN#ixzz1lNVVyvHl.
30. Ibid.
31. K. Crowley, "Charity Big Probed over Pay," *New York Post*, May 23, 2011, http://www.nypost.com/p/news/local/charity_big_probed_over_pay_022DUuafqsoQt96OrntBGL.
32. Crowley, "Head of AIDS Charity Complaining."
33. Ibid.
34. *Illinois ex rel. Madigan, Attorney General of Illinois* v. *Telemarketing Associates, Inc., et al.*, no. 01–1806, U.S. Supreme Court, May 5, 2003, p. 18; *Randolph Riley, etc., et al.* v. *National Federation of the Blind of North Carolina, Inc., et al.*, no. 87–328, U.S. Supreme Court, June 29, 1988.
35. D. L. Wabnik, letter to Edward P. Mangano and George Maragos, "Re: Response by Board of Directors of Long Island Association for AIDS Care to the Nassau County Comptroller Press Release Regarding Long Island Association for AIDS Care," May 24, 2011, http://www.liaac.org/images/pubs/press/press_5_24_11.pdf.
36. R. Buettner, "Reaping Millions in Nonprofit Care for Disabled," *New York Times*, Aug. 2, 2011, http://www.nytimes.com/2011/08/02/nyregion/for-executives-at-group-homes-generous-pay-and-little-oversight.html?pagewanted=all.
37. R. Buettner, "State Panel to Review Pay of Leaders at Nonprofits," *New York Times*, Aug. 3, 2011, http://cityroom.blogs.nytimes.com/2011/08/03/pay-for-heads-of-nonprofit-groups-will-be-scrutinized/.

38. Ibid.
39. Office of the New York State Comptroller Response to Freedom of Information Request 2011–476 for the "total amount of awarded contracts for not-for-profits compared to for-profit contracts in 2010 or the most recent year available," Sept. 25, 2011.
40. "New York Governor Andrew Cuomo Orders Investigation of Nonprofit Exec Pay," *Huffington Post*, Aug. 5, 2011, http://www.wopular.com/new-york-governor-andrew-cuomo-orders-investigation-nonprofit-exec-pay.
41. Buettner, "State Panel to Review Pay of Leaders at Nonprofits."
42. "New York Governor Andrew Cuomo Orders Investigation of Nonprofit Exec Pay," *Huffington Post*, Aug. 5, 2011, http://www.huffingtonpost.com/2011/08/05/new-york-governor-andrew-_n_919642.html.
43. Ibid.
44. Ibid.
45. Buettner, "State Panel to Review Pay of Leaders at Nonprofits."
46. R. Buettner, "State Seeks Data on Pay of Leaders at Nonprofits," *New York Times*, Aug. 25, 2011, http://www.nytimes.com/2011/08/26/nyregion/state-seeks-data-on-pay-of-leaders-at-nonprofits.html?_r=1.
47. Ibid.
48. Buettner, "State Seeks Data on Pay of Leaders at Nonprofits."
49. M. Fisher, "MoCo Strikes Back at D.C. Charity's Big Spending," *Washington Post*, June 4, 2009, http://voices.washingtonpost.com/rawfisher/2009/05/moco_strikes_back_at_dc_charit.html.
50. P. Rucker, "Chief's Pay Criticized as Charity Cuts Back," *Washington Post*, July 17, 2008, http://www.washingtonpost.com/wp-dyn/content/article/2008/07/16/AR2008071602658.html.
51. Ibid.
52. Fisher.
53. Ibid.
54. Ibid.
55. A. Kredo, "What Is 'Too Much'? Decision to Revoke Charity's Grant Questioned," *Washington Jewish Week*, May 27, 2009, http://www.washingtonjewishweek.com/print.asp?ArticleID=10851&SectionID=4&SubSectionID=53.
56. Ibid.

57. In February 2012, that Web site had different wording. See "Charity CEO Pay Pt. 2," *Charity Navigator's YouTube Channel*, May 27, 2009, http://www.youtube.com/user/CharityNavigator#p/u/1/TDy7TXGmAcE, accessed Feb. 2012.
58. M. Blumberg, "How Does a Canadian Charity Determine Appropriate Compensation for an Executive of the Charity?" What's New from the Charities Directorate of CRA, Canadian Charity Law, Fundraising Guidance for Registered Charities, http://www.canadiancharitylaw.ca/index.php/blog/comments/how_does_a_canadian_charity_determine_appropriate_compensation_for_an_execu/, accessed Feb. 8, 2012
59. U.S. Department of the Treasury, Internal Revenue Service, "Form 990-PF: Return of Private Foundation or Section 4947(a)(1) Nonexempt Charitable Trust Treated as a Private Foundation," filing organization: Charity Navigator, Glen Rock, N.J., filing year: 2009, http://www.guidestar.org/FinDocuments//2010/134/148/2010-134148824-0736c584-F.pdf.
60. U.S. Department of the Treasury, Internal Revenue Service, "Form 990: Return of Organization Exempt from Income Tax," filing organization: American Institute of Philanthropy, Chicago, filing year: 2010, http://www.guidestar.org/FinDocuments//2010/330/491/2010-330491030-07422dec-9.pdf.
61. Rucker.
62. Food & Friends, *2009 Annual Report*, http://www.foodandfriends.org/atf/cf/%7B7C8C5560-FF18-46CD-B907-B7EFBF2114DC%7D/116986_report.pdf.
63. GLAAD (Gay & Lesbian Alliance Against Defamation), "Homepage," July 6, 2011, http://www.glaad.org/, accessed July 6, 2011.
64. GLAAD (Gay & Lesbian Alliance Against Defamation), "About," July 6, 2011, http://www.glaad.org/about, accessed July 6, 2011.
65. Ibid.
66. Ibid.
67. AYP Gay and Lesbian Business Directory, "View Category List—Organizations—GLAAD (Gay & Lesbians Alliance Against Defamation)" Feb. 2012, http://www.ayptampa.com/index.php?option=com_sobi2&sobi2Task=sobi2Details&catid=268&sobi2Id=2742&Itemid=45, accessed Feb. 2012.

68. C. Franklin, "Gay Marriage Support and Opposition," *Pollster*, May 21, 2008, http://www.pollster.com/blogs/gay_marriage_support_and_oppos.php?nr=1. Gallup Poll, "Gay and Lesbian Rights," Feb. 2012, http://www.gallup.com/poll/1651/Gay-Lesbian-Rights.aspx#1, accessed Feb. 2012.
69. K. Bowman, "Attitudes About Homosexuality and Gay Marriage," *AEI Studies in Public Opinion*, June 3, 2008, http://www.aei.org/files/2008/06/03/20080603-Homosexuality.pdf. L. Morales, "In U.S., Broad, Steady Support for Openly Gay Service Members," *Gallup Politics*, May 10, 2010, http://www.gallup.com/poll/127904/broad-steady-support-openly-gay-service-members.aspx.
70. U.S Department of the Treasury, Internal Revenue Service, "Form 990: Return of Organization Exempt from Income Tax," filing organization: Gay and Lesbian Alliance Against Defamation, Los Angeles, filing year: 2009, http://www.guidestar.org/FinDocuments//2009/133/384/2009-133384027-065022ab-9.pdf.
71. U.S Department of the Treasury, Internal Revenue Service, "Form 990: Return of Organization Exempt from Income Tax," filing organization: Independent Sector, Washington, D.C., filing year: 2010, http://www.independentsector.org/uploads/About_IS/Key_Documents/IS2010-12TAXForm990PublicDisclosureCopy.pdf.
72. Independent Sector, "Mission, Vision, and Values," http://www.independentsector.org/mission_and_values, accessed Feb. 2012.
73. Department of the Treasury, Internal Revenue Service, "Form 990: Return of Organization Exempt from Income Tax," filing organization: Human Rights Campaign Inc., Washington, D.C., filing year: 2009, http://www.guidestar.org/FinDocuments/2010/521/243/2010-521243457-066c8c8d-9O.pdf.
74. National Gay and Lesbian Task Force, "*2010 Annual Report*," http://www.thetaskforce.org/downloads/devo/ar_2010_interactive.pdf, accessed Feb. 2012.
75. Lambda Legal, *2010 Annual Report*, http://www.lambdalegal.org/sites/default/files/publications/downloads/ar_2010_making-the-case-for-equality_1.pdf, accessed Feb. 2012.
76. Department of the Treasury, Internal Revenue Service, "Form 990: Return of Organization Exempt from Income Tax," filing organization: Parents,

Families, and Friends of Lesbians and Gays, Inc., Washington, D.C., filing year: 2009, http://issuu.com/dmanuel/docs/pflag990_2009?mode=embed&viewMode=presentation&layout=http%3A%2F%2Fskin.issuu.com%2Fv%2Flight%2Flayout.xml&showFlipBtn=true.

77. Anti-Defamation League, *2009 Annual Report*, http://www.adl.org/annual_report/Annual_Report_2009.pdf, accessed Feb. 2012.
78. National Association for the Advancement of Colored People, *2009 Annual Report*, http://naacp.3cdn.net/99f25becef37ea9364_v6m6i48q8.pdf, accessed Feb. 2012.
79. R. Cohen, "Proposed Federal Bill to Focus on the Needs of Nonprofits," *Nonprofit Quarterly*, June 16, 2010, http://www.nonprofitquarterly.org/index.php?option=com_content&view=article&id=3081.
80. U.S. Department of Labor, Bureau of Labor Statistics, "Employment Situation Summary Table A. Household Data, Seasonally Adjusted," Feb. 3, 2012, http://www.bls.gov/news.release/empsit.a.htm.
81. R. Ptacek, *NBC Action News*, personal interview by author, July 22, 2011.
82. B. Zlatos, *Pittsburgh Tribune-Review*, personal interview by author, July 29, 2011.
83. Ptacek.
84. E. Ailworth, *Boston Globe*, personal interview by author, Aug. 31, 2011.
85. Ibid.
86. B. Healey, *Boston Globe*, personal interview by author, Aug. 18, 2011.
87. Ptacek.
88. Zlatos, interview.
89. Ibid.
90. Healey, interview.
91. Ailworth, interview.

Chapter Three

1. M. Ramsey and K. Linebaugh, "Early Tests Pin Toyota Accidents on Drivers," *Wall Street Journal*, July 13, 2010, http://online.wsj.com/article/SB10001424052748703834604575364871534435744.html.
2. U.S. Department of the Treasury, Internal Revenue Service, "Form 990: Return of Organization Exempt from Income Tax," filing organization:

Save the Children Federation Inc., Westport, Conn., filing year: 2009, http://www.guidestar.org/FinDocuments//2009/060/726/2009-060726487-0662de79-9.pdf.

3. Advertising Age, "DATA: 100 Leading National Advertisers, 2011 Edition," http://adage.com/datacenter/datapopup.php?article_id=228228, accessed Feb. 2012.
4. Department of the Treasury, Internal Revenue Service, "Form 990: Return of Organization Exempt from Income Tax," filing organization: Save the Children Federation Inc., Westport, Conn., filing year: 2009, http://www.guidestar.org/FinDocuments//2009/060/726/2009-060726487-0662de79-9.pdf.
5. Walt Disney Company, *2010 Annual Financial Report and Shareholder Letter*, http://amedia.disney.go.com/investorrelations/annual_reports/WDC-10kwrap-2010.pdf?int_cmp=corp_IR_ARview_link1__Intll, accessed Feb. 2012.
6. S. Elliott, "Egg Industry Comes out of Its Old-Media Shell," *New York Times*, Nov. 5, 2007, http://www.nytimes.com/2007/11/05/business/media/05adnewsletter1.html?adxnnl=1&adxnnlx=1328396612-rNXEUFPgC9ECtqe0obC28A.
7. American Egg Board, "AEB Mission," http://www.aeb.org/about-aeb/mission, accessed Feb. 2012.
8. Incredibly Edible Egg, "Home," http://www.incredibleegg.org/, accessed Feb. 2012.
9. Incredibly Edible Egg, "For Big Days," http://www.incredibleegg.org/whats-on-tv/for-big-days-commercials, accessed Feb. 2012.
10. American Egg Board, *Annual Report*, http://www.aeb.org/images/website/documents/about-aeb/annual-report/annual-report_2010.pdf, p. 16, accessed Feb. 2012.
11. Ibid., p. 9.
12. Ibid., p. 7.
13. Incredible Edible Egg Facebook page, https://www.facebook.com/IncredibleEdibleEgg?sk=app_158072797586019, accessed Feb. 2012.
14. Pork Be Inspired, "The Other White Meat Brand," http://www.porkbeinspired.com/towm_promo_heritage_page.aspx, accessed Feb. 2012.
15. Ibid.

16. J. J. Putnam and J. E. Allshouse, "Food Consumption," in *Food Consumption, Prices, and Expenditures, 1970–97* (Washington, D.C.: U.S. Department of Agriculture, 1999), p. 18, http://www.ers.usda.gov/publications/sb965/sb965f.pdf.
17. T. Hall, "And This Little Piggy Is Now on the Menu," *New York Times*, Nov. 13, 1991, http://www.nytimes.com/1991/11/13/garden/and-this-little-piggy-is-now-on-the-menu.html.
18. Center on Philanthropy at Indiana University, *Giving USA 2008: The Annual Report on Philanthropy for the Year 2008* (Bloomington, Ind.: Giving USA Foundation, 2009), p. 15.
19. Ibid.
20. Pork Be Inspired, "Find Recipes, Cooking Ideas, Pork History and More," http://www.porkbeinspired.com/Index.aspx, accessed Feb. 2012.
21. Pork Be Inspired Facebook page, https://www.facebook.com/PorkBeInspired, accessed Feb. 2012.
22. Y. Noguchi, "Slick Oil Ads Aim to Bolster Industry's Image," National Public Radio, June 20, 2008, http://www.npr.org/templates/story/story.php?storyId=9170017.
23. American Petroleum Institute, "About API," http://www.api.org/aboutapi/ads/index.cfm, accessed Aug. 17, 2011.
24. R. Lefton and N. Nielsen, "Interactive: Big Polluters' Big Ad Spending," Center for American Progress Action Fund, Oct. 27, 2010, http://www.americanprogressaction.org/issues/2010/10/bigoilmoney.html.
25. Energy Tomorrow Facebook page, http://www.facebook.com/Energy.Tomorrow, accessed Feb. 2012.
26. J. Steel, *Truth, Lies, and Advertising: The Art of Account Planning* (Hoboken, N.J.: Wiley, 1998), p. 233. B. Horovitz, "Meet the Milk Man: No, He Doesn't Like to Drink It. But Jeff Goodby Sure Can Sell It. Could It Be That Milk Will Become—Gulp—a Hip Drink?" *Los Angeles Times*, May 27, 1994, p. 2, http://articles.latimes.com/1994-05-27/news/ls-62963_1_milk-ad. J. Manning, *Got Milk?* (New York: Prima Publishing, 1999), p. 6.
27. Manning, p. 11.
28. Ibid., p. 38.
29. Ibid.
30. Ibid.

31. Horovitz, p. 3.
32. Steel, p. 265.
33. Ibid.
34. Ibid.
35. Ibid.
36. Ibid.
37. Ibid.
38. D. Borenstein, "Milk: 'Got Milk?' Article," *Milk*, http://www.milk.com/value/innovator-spring99.html, accessed Feb. 2012.
39. B. Sunset, "Got Milk? Campaign," *Marketing Campaign Case Studies* (blog), Apr. 21, 2008, http://marketing-case-studies.blogspot.com/2008/04/got-milk-campaign.html.
40. Got Milk? Facebook page, http://www.facebook.com/gotmilk, accessed Feb. 2012.
41. J. K. Owyang, J. Bernoff, T. Cummings, and E. Bowen, "Social Media Playtime Is Over: Despite the Recession, More Than 50% of Marketers Will Pursue Social Applications," Forrester Research, Mar. 16, 2009, p. 1, http://www.forrester.com/rb/Research/social_media_playtime_is_over/q/id/47665/t/2.
42. "Corporate Social Media Spend to Increase Among B2B Companies Globally According to Worldcom Survey," Worldcom B2B media release, May 11, 2011, http://www.worldcomprgroupemea.com/social-media/corporate-social-media-spend-to-increase-among-b2b-companies-globally-according-to-worldcom-survey/.
43. CMO Survey, "Topline Results" (Durham, N.C.: CMO Survey, Aug. 2011), http://cmosurvey.org/files/2011/08/Topline-Results-Aug-2011_Final.pdf.
44. S. Hudson, "Few Charities Raise Significant Funds on Facebook," *Third Sector*, Oct. 19, 2011, http://www.thirdsector.co.uk/news/1099428/.
45. R. Flandez, "Most Charities Still Do Not Raise Much Money via Social Media," *Chronicle of Philanthropy*, Aug. 21, 2011, http://philanthropy.com/article/Big-Charities-Gear-Up-to-Use/128741/.
46. Ibid.

Chapter Four

1. D. K. Row, "Not-So-Giving Charities Would Be Punished Under Bill in Oregon Legislature," *Oregonian*, Mar. 16, 2011, http://www.oregonlive

.com/pacific-northwest-news/index.ssf/2011/03/bad_charities_would_be_punished_under_bill_in_oregon_legislature.html.

2. R. K. Merton, "The Unanticipated Consequences of Purposive Social Action," *American Sociological Review*, 1936, *1*, 894–904, http://www.jstor.org/stable/2084615, p. 894.
3. R. K. Merton, "The Unanticipated Consequences of Social Action," in P. Sztompka (Ed.), *On Social Structure and Science* (Chicago: University of Chicago Press, 1996), p. 177.
4. Ibid, p. 178.
5. Ibid., p. 179.
6. Ibid, p. 180.
7. Ibid., p. 185.
8. Center on Nonprofits and Philanthropy, Urban Institute at the Center on Philanthropy at Indiana University, "What We Know About Overhead Costs in the Nonprofit Sector," *Nonprofit Overhead Cost Project: Facts and Perspectives*, brief no. 1 (Feb. 2004), p. 1.
9. G. Peters to D. Pallotta, memorandum, Sept. 29, 2011, p. 4.
10. *Illinois ex rel. Madigan, Attorney General of Illinois* v. *Telemarketing Associates, Inc., et al.*, no. 01–1806, U.S. Supreme Court, May 5, 2003, p. 18.
11. *Randolph Riley, etc., et al.* v. *National Federation of the Blind of North Carolina, Inc., et al.*, no. 87–328, U.S. Supreme Court, June 29, 1988.
12. *Secretary of State of Maryland* v. *Joseph H. Munson Co., Inc.*, no. 82–766, U.S. Supreme Court, June 26, 1984, via Lexis-Nexis, http://web.lexis-nexis.com, accessed June 30, 2006.
13. *Randolph Riley, etc., et al.* v. *National Federation of the Blind of North Carolina.*
14. Row.
15. J. Wynn and others, "Mortality in Achondroplasia Study: A 42-Year Follow-Up," *American Journal of Medical Genetics Part A*, 2007, *143A*, 2502–2511, accessed Feb. 7, 2012.
16. Better Business Bureau, "Standards for Charity Accountability," 2003, http://www.bbb.org/us/Charity-Standards/, accessed Feb. 2012.
17. D. K. Row, " Senate Bill 40, Intended to Punish Bad Charities, May Die in the Oregon House," *Oregonian*, May 31, 2011, http://www.oregonlive.com/pacific-northwest-news/index.ssf/2011/05/senate_bill_40_intended.html.

18. Ibid.
19. Senate Standing Committee on Investigations and Government Operations, "Public Hearing: To Examine Executive Compensation at Not-for-Profit Organizations Receiving State Funding and the Actions Needed to Prevent State Tax Dollars from Being Wasted on Excessive Salaries," Jan. 26, 2012, press release, http://63.118.56.3/lbdcinfo/senpublichearing.html.
20. See ThroughNY, "Payrolls," 2010, http://seethroughny.net/payrolls/, accessed Feb. 2012.
21. Division of the Budget, New York State Office of the Governor, *2012–13 Execute Budget and Reform Plan: New NY Transformation Plan . . . The Next Step*, Jan. 17, 2012, p. 14, http://publications.budget.ny.gov/eBudget1213/fy1213littlebook/BriefingBook.pdf, accessed Feb. 2012.
22. J. Berkshire, "Charity Workers Report Feeling Extreme Pressure," *Chronicle of Philanthropy*, Jan. 19, 2012, p. 15.
23. G. Peters to D. M. Pallotta, memorandum, "Litigation That American Charities for Reasonable Fundraising Regulation Could/Should Have Pursued If Resources Were Sufficient," Sept. 13, 2011, p. 2.
24. U.S. Department of the Treasury, Internal Revenue Service, "Form 990: Return of Organization Exempt from Income Tax," filing organization: Disability Rights Education and Defense Fund, Berkeley, Calif., filing year: 2008, http://www.guidestar.org/FinDocuments//2009/942/620/2009-942620758-0650f2e0-9.pdf.
25. NAACP Legal Defense and Education Fund, "History," http://www.naacpldf.org/history, accessed Feb. 2012.
26. U.S. Department of the Treasury, Internal Revenue Service, "Form 990: Return of Organization Exempt from Income Tax," filing organization: NAACP Legal Defense and Education Fund, New York, N.Y., filing year: 2009, http://www.guidestar.org/FinDocuments/2010/131/655/2010-131655255-06d0fc85-9.pdf.
27. Asian American Legal Defense and Education Fund, *Biennial Report 2009–2010*, http://aaldef.org/2009-10%20biennial%20report.pdf, accessed Feb. 2012.
28. U.S. Department of the Treasury, Internal Revenue Service, "Form 990: Return of Organization Exempt from Income Tax," filing organization:

Maldef, Los Angeles, filing year: 2009, http://www.guidestar.org/FinDocuments/2010/741/563/2010-741563270-07018b2e-9.pdf.

29. U.S. Department of the Treasury, Internal Revenue Service, "Form 990-EZ: Return of Organization Exempt from Income Tax," filing organization: American Charities for Reasonable Fundraising Regulation Inc, Vienna, Va., filing year: 2007, http://www.guidestar.org/FinDocuments/2007/223/096/2007-223096395-06400280-Z.pdf.
30. G. Peters, e-mail message to D. M. Pallotta, Sept. 29, 2011.
31. Ibid.
32. *American Charities for Reasonable Fundraising Regulation, Inc., Creative Advantage, Inc., et al., Plaintiffs-Appellants,* v. *Pinellas County, a Political Subdivision of the State of Florida, Nugent Walsh, As Chairperson of the Charitable Solicitations Board of Pinellas County, et al.*, Defendants-Appellees, no. 221, F.3d 1211, U.S. Court of Appeals for the Eleventh Circuit, Aug. 10, 2000, http://law.justia.com/cases/federal/appellate-courts/F3/221/1211/526371/.
33. Peters to Pallotta, memorandum, Sept. 29, 2011, p. 10.
34. Florida Department of Agriculture and Consumer Services, Division of Consumer Services, "Solicitation of Contributions," http://www.800helpfla.com/soc.html, accessed Feb. 2012.
35. *American Charities for Reasonable Fundraising Regulation, Inc.*, v. *Pinellas County*.
36. Ibid.
37. "American Charities for Reasonable Fundraising Regulation," Apr. 1998, http://www.muridae.com/nporegulation/documents/acfrfr_flyer.html, accessed Feb. 2012.
38. Ibid.
39. *American Charities for Reasonable Fundraising Regulation* v. *Pinellas County*.
40. Ibid.
41. Peters to Pallotta, memorandum, Sept. 29, 2011, p. 11.
42. American Charities for Reasonable Fundraising Regulation, "Combating Excessive Regulation of Nonprofits and Fundraising by Means of Litigation," http://www.charityreg.org/faqs.html, accessed Feb. 2012.
43. Ibid.

44. G. Peters to D. M. Pallotta, memorandum, "American Charities for Reasonable Fundraising Regulation Background & Litigation History," Sept. 13, 2011, p. 1.
45. Ibid., p. 4.
46. American Charities for Reasonable Fundraising Regulation, "Combating Excessive Regulation."
47. Ibid.
48. State of New Jersey, Department of Law & Public Safety, Division of Consumer Affairs, "Rule Proposal: Notice of Pre-Proposal Disclosures to the Public," Vol. 43, Issue 11, http://www.state.nj.us/lps/ca/proposal/charpro_060611.htm, accessed Feb. 6, 2012.
49. E. Copilevitz, draft of letter to T. Calcagni, acting director, New Jersey Division of Consumer Affairs, July 16, 2011.
50. Los Angeles Police Commission, Division of Charitable Services Section, "Notice of Intention to Solicit Charitable Contributions," Dec. 2011, http://www.lapdonline.org/police_commission/content_basic_view/9152#documents, accessed Feb. 2012.
51. Ibid.
52. Los Angeles Police Department, "Frequently Asked Questions About Charitable Organizations," http://www.lapdonline.org/police_commission/content_basic_view/9152#documents, accessed Feb. 2012.
53. Los Angeles Police Department, "Information Card," http://www.lapdonline.org/police_commission/content_basic_view/9148, accessed Feb. 2012. Los Angeles Police Commission. Division of Charitable Services Section, Commission Investigation Division, "Information Card C0001," Mar. 20, 2009.
54. *Randolph Riley et al.* v. *National Federation of the Blind of North Carolina.*
55. Los Angeles Police Commission, Division of Charitable Services Section, "Report of Results of Activity" (PDF), Jan. 2001, http://www.lapdonline.org/police_commission/content_basic_view/9152#documents, accessed Feb. 2012.
56. Ibid.
57. *Illinois ex rel. Madigan, Attorney General of Illinois* v. *Telemarketing Associates, Inc., et al.*, no. 01–1806, U.S. Supreme Court, May 5, 2003, p. 18.

58. Peters to Pallotta, memorandum, Sept. 29, 2011, p. 16.
59. *Gospel Missions* v. *City of Los Angeles*, no. 00–55993, U.S. Court of Appeals for the Ninth Circuit, Aug. 8, 2002, http://www.charityreg.org/downloads/Other/Gospel_Missions.pdf.
60. *Gospel Missions* v. *City of Los Angeles*, no. 00–55993, U.S. Court of Appeals for the Ninth Circuit, Au. 17, 2005, from http://caselaw.findlaw.com/us-9th-circuit/1244814.html.
61. *Gospel Missions* v. *City of Los Angeles*, no. 00–55993, U.S. Court of Appeals for the Ninth Circuit, Aug. 8, 2002, http://www.charityreg.org/downloads/Other/Gospel_Missions.pdf.
62. *Gospel Missions* v. *City of Los Angeles*, no. 00–55993, United States Court of Appeals for the Ninth Circuit, Aug. 17, 2005, http://caselaw.findlaw.com/us-9th-circuit/1244814.html.
63. *Gospel Missions* v. *City of Los Angeles*, no. 00–55993, U.S. Court of Appeals for the Ninth Circuit, Aug. 8, 2002, from http://www.charityreg.org/downloads/Other/Gospel_Missions.pdf.
64. G. W. Moore, State Representative, House District 50, Tennessee General Assembly, House Bill no. 1135, Public Chapter No. 232, May 25, 2011, http://www.tn.gov/sos/acts/107/pub/pc0232.pdf, accessed Feb. 2012. Tennessee Department of State, Division of Charitable Solicitations and Gaming, "Charitable Fundraising & Gaming," http://www.tn.gov/sos/charity/, accessed Feb. 2012.
65. Tennessee Department of State, Division of Charitable Solicitations and Gaming, *Disaster Relief Fundraising Quarterly Financial Report*, http://www.tn.gov/sos/forms/ss-6082.pdf, accessed Feb. 2012.
66. Tennessee Department of State, Division of Charitable Solicitations and Gaming, "Financial Reports for Registered Charities," http://tnsos.org/charitable/CharitableOrgReports.php, accessed Feb. 2012.
67. Peters to Pallotta, memorandum, Sept. 29, 2011, p. 18.
68. Tennessee Department of State, Division of Charitable Solicitations and Gaming, "Financial Reports for Registered Charities."
69. M. Peltier and M. Menzel, "Bill Would Cap Non-Profit Salaries," *Jacksonville Business Journal*, Jan. 27, 2012.
70. Peters to Pallotta, memorandum, Sept. 29, 2011, p. 19.
71. Ibid.

72. From the first bullet of page 31 to here: Peters to Pallotta, memorandum, "Litigation."
73. Ibid.

Chapter Five

1. U.S. Internal Revenue Service, "Exemption Requirements—Section 501(c)(3) Organizations," Jan. 30, 2012, http://www.irs.gov/charities/charitable/article/0,,id=96099,00.html.
2. N. Johnson, P. Oliff, and E. Williams, "An Update on State Budget Cuts: At Least 46 States Have Imposed Cuts That Hurt Vulnerable Residents and the Economy," Center on Budget and Policy Priorities, Feb. 9, 2011, http://www.cbpp.org/cms/index.cfm?fa=view&id=1214.
3. B. Greenstein, "Grim Budget Realities and Their Implications for Americans of Lesser Means" (slide 14, presentation to Independent Sector), Sept. 13, 2011.
4. Ibid. U.S. Census, "Income, Poverty, and Health Insurance Coverage in the US, 2010," Sept. 13, 2011, http://www.census.gov/newsroom/releases/archives/income_wealth/cb11-157.html.
5. E. T. Boris, E. de Leon, K. Roeger, and M. Nikolova, "Human Service Nonprofits and Government Collaboration: Findings from the 2010 National Survey of Nonprofit Government Contracting and Grants," Urban Institute, Oct. 2010, http://www.urban.org/uploadedpdf/412228-Nonprofit-Government-Contracting.pdf.
6. Ibid.
7. G. L. Keohane, "Philanthropy and the Social Contract: What Comes Next," Center for Effective Philanthropy, Feb. 5, 2010, http://www.effectivephilanthropy.org/blog/author/georgialk/.

Chapter Six

1. Alcoholics Anonymous, "Estimates of A.A. Groups and Members," Jan. 1, 2011, http://www.aa.org/subpage.cfm?page=74.

Chapter Seven

1. M. O'Brien and J. King, "Bush Unveils Vision for Moon and Beyond," Cable News Network, Jan. 15, 2005, http://articles.cnn.com/2004-01-14

/tech/bush.space_1_space-exploration-mars-mission-human-missions?_s=PM:TECH.

2. John F. Kennedy, "Special Message to Congress on Urgent National Needs," May 25, 1961, http://www.jfklibrary.org/Asset-Viewer/xzw1gaeeTES6KhED14P1lw.aspx.
3. P. C. Light, "How Americans View Charities: A Report on Charitable Confidence, 2008" (Washington, D.C.: Brookings Institution, Apr. 2008), http://www.brookings.edu/papers/2008/04_nonprofits_light.asp.

Thank You

This book has just one name on the cover, but it was made possible by many generous spirits, great thinkers, and friends.

I first want to thank John Schneider, Ellen Wicklum, and everyone else at Tufts University Press for believing in my book *Uncharitable* when no one else did. This book owes its life to that one.

Stephanie Tade is my book agent, but she's also been my sounding board and a writing mentor for the last five years. *Uncharitable* was initially a book exclusively about overhead ratios. It was Stephanie who challenged me to dig deeper and write about the ideology that lies at their root. Once I did, and decided it was founded in Puritan ethos, it was she who challenged me again: How do you know that? Which led to a six-month intensive study of Puritan history. Without those challenges, *Uncharitable* would never have been the book it is, and *Charity Case* would never have come into being. Stephanie played a similar role with this book, guiding and pointing the way during the journey.

Genoveva Llosa is my editor at Jossey-Bass. This is the first book we've worked on together. How did I get so lucky? What you hope for as a writer is a partnership with someone who cares as much about the work as you do. That wish came true with Genoveva. Her heart has been in this book from the start. Her enthusiasm, candor, and commitment were unrelenting. She was determined that this book attract the widest possible audience and have the greatest possible impact. It's rare that you get to work with someone whose motivations are that pure and aligned with your own.

Ali Megdhadi is a Ph.D. candidate at the University of California at Irvine in the Department of Comparative Literature. He is also my friend and an exceptional researcher and editor. Excellence and attention to detail matter to him in every argument, statistic, source, citation, quotation, endnote, and bracket. We became friends working many, many long hours together on *Uncharitable*, and I have come to trust him with research and editing more than I trust myself. It's impossible to quantify the comfort that comes with knowing he'll be on a project with me. His standards are impeccable, and his smarts are off the charts—a rare combination.

Geoffrey Peters made Chapter Four possible. He contributed argument, content, case histories, and a thoughtful review of the finished product. I would not have felt comfortable including the chapter without his work. He is a tireless fighter for our sector and an expert on fundraising law and public policy with few peers. We need many more like him.

George O'Har is a full-time adjunct faculty member in the English Department at Boston College, where he teaches courses on literature and technology, utopia, creative writing, and creative nonfiction. He also happens to be my uncle. He can hold an entire book in his mind at once and make big-picture structural and editing decisions with a clarity that eludes mere mortals and authors who have gotten too close to their project. As he did with *Uncharitable*, George lent his genius to the final product when we needed to get the word count down substantially without losing any of the substance of the arguments. He saved every reader at least an hour and a half of unnecessary reading.

Irv Warner was my mentor and friend. He taught me everything I know about fundraising. Irv passed away while this book was being written. It would not exist but for his having lived and cared so deeply about social justice and making this world a more humane place.

I would also like to acknowledge and thank the following people:

Errol Copilevitz, for helping Geoffrey and me on Chapter Four and for his general magnanimity; everyone who contributed an essay to Chapter Five—Cass Brewer, Lawrence Mendenhall, George Overholser, Errol Copilevitz, Billy Shore, Diana Aviv, Bob Ottenhoff, Paul Grogan, Jennifer Aronson, Eric Walker, John Tyler, Geoffrey Peters, Leslie Lenkowsky, Marc Lane, Alex Alvanos, Bob Lang, and Art Taylor; Sara Howell for being the world's greatest assistant; Rex Wilder for a smart title; John Carlos Harrington and Paiwei Wei for their powerful jacket composition ideas and the "I'm overhead" ads; Denny Chen for his figure graphics; Paiwei Wei for being my friend and for the great Web site design for "Uncharitable" that has generated so much interest in building a movement for change and Ben Stanley for helping maintain the site; Mark Stanton and the team at Advertising for Humanity for protecting time for me to write; Andrew Filippone Jr. for the documentary work on my talks and Bryn Mathieu for the documentary audio; everyone at Jossey-Bass who has had a hand in making this real, most of whom I haven't met, in sales, marketing, editing, promotions, communications, and production; Katherine Bell, Christina Bortz, Jenny Davidson, Peter Diamandis, Sasha Dichter, Michael Fairbanks, Jonathan Graspas, Jane Pak, Kathleen Paylor, Billy Shore, Debbie Shore, Rich Tafel, and Brian Trelstad for title advice; Seth Perlman for feeding me news; the reporters I interviewed who were willing to have the tables turned on them; the American Program Bureau, especially Nancy Eisenstein, Melissa Abrahams, and Holly Goulet; Camille McDuffie and Angela Hayes at Goldberg McDuffie for helping me get my books on the road and in the news; everyone who hosted a talk on *Uncharitable* (you got this movement started); everyone who came to a talk and offered their enthusiasm and support; and Tad and Jorge at Made to Order for the "I'm overhead" shirts. Thanks to all who have agreed to serve on the advisory board for the Charity Defense Council, including Seth Perlman, Peter Diamandis, Milton Little, Tamara Copeland, Billy Shore, Jerr Boschee, and Art Taylor.

Thanks to my children, Annalisa, Sage, and Rider Smith-Pallotta, who inspire me every day. You will read this book someday when you are older. You are the real reason I care about how the world thinks about making a difference, because I want you to grow up in a very different kind of world.

Last but not least, Jimmy Smith is my spouse, my partner, my best friend, and the love of my life. He reads my books more than I do. He keeps my enthusiasm and motivation going when the going gets tough. And he keeps the kids out of the room while I'm trying to think.

About the Author

Dan Pallotta is a builder of movements. He created the multi-day charitable event industry with the AIDSRides, Breast Cancer 3-Days, and Out of the Darkness suicide prevention events. These events challenged participants to journey long distances for multiple days in the name of causes they cared about deeply. More than 182,000 people rode or walked in these events, which raised $582 million in nine years and were the subject of a Harvard Business School case study. His ideas are now used on dozens of multi-day charitable events that have raised in excess of $1 billion for important causes.

He is the author of *Uncharitable*, which the *Stanford Social Innovation Review* said "deserves to become the nonprofit sector's new manifesto." It has shifted the national conversation about the role of nonprofit organizations and the rules by which they must play. He is a featured contributor to *Harvard Business Review* online, where he writes about social innovation. He is president of Advertising for Humanity, a bold agency of ideas bringing world-class marketing acumen to the most urgent causes of our time.

Dan is a 1983 graduate of Harvard University. He was elected to the school board in Melrose, Massachusetts, at age twenty. He is the founder of the Charity Defense Council, a board member of Triangle, a center for the developmentally disabled, and a member of the Reason Project advisory board. He is a recipient of the Liberty Hill Foundation Creative Vision award, the Triangle Humanitarian of the Year award, the Albany State University International Citizen of the Year award, and the Seven Fund's Morality of Profit Essay Prize. He is a William J. Clinton Distinguished Lecturer and has spoken at Stanford, Wharton, Harvard, NASA, the Gates Foundation, the Hewlett Foundation, Google, and the Milken Institute, among others.

He lives in Massachusetts with his partner and their three children.

Index